noodle

Terry Durack

photography by Geoff Lung

SOMA
San Francisco

contents

Long Life and Happiness	iv
Noodle Survival: How to Use this Book	1
Noodle ID	2
China	44
China–Beijing	48
China–Chiu Chow	51
China–Guangdong	52
China–Far North	64
China–Shanghai	66
China–Sichuan	71
China–Yunan	78
China–Modern	79
Noodle Tale 1: Long-Life Noodles	88
Japan	90
Japan–Modern	109
Malaysia	112
Malaysia–Modern	125
Noodle Tale 2: Noodle Love	126
Thailand	128
Thailand–Modern	140
Vietnam	144
Korea	156
Noodle Tale 3: Word of Mouth	166
Indonesia	170
Philippines	173
Burma	174
Taiwan	176
Laos	178
Cambodia	179
India	180
Noodle Tale 4: Crossing the Bridge	182
Basics	184
Glossary	194
Bibliography	198
Index	199

Long Life and Happiness

To witness the birth of a noodle is a glorious thing.

I have listened, spellbound, as an 85-year-old noodle chef in Beijing told me why the act of making noodles helped him make sense of the world. As he spoke, he effortlessly stretched a soft, white blob of dough into a thick skipping-rope affair that began to dance before my eyes. It twirled and furled and stretched and strained until he deftly passed one end of the dough to his other hand, causing the rope to twist upon itself.

Back and forth he folded the rope upon itself until for no reason apparent to mere earthlings, it split into noodles. A little twist and it splits into even finer noodles. And so it went, until the man had produced noodles so fine they could pass through the eye of a needle.

I have watched Mongolian noodle-makers slam their hand-pulled noodles so hard on their work tables that I feared the wood would splinter. I have witnessed master soba chef Yoshi Shibazaki push and prod and roll his buckwheat dough until he was weak with the effort.

I have watched antique machines in outer suburbia steaming rough mixes of rice flour and water until they turned into a bridal white, gelatinous dough that is then stretched into shimmering silken sheets, cooled by rattly old fans hanging from the ceiling.

I have plunged my hands—well, my whole body—into flour in an effort to make my own noodles, ending up with a snow-white kitchen and a small bowl full of the most satisfying noodles in the world.

To all the people who create the noodles of the world, I dedicate this book.

I also make them a pledge: to treat their noodles with the same care, respect, and integrity that they have shown by making them in the first place.

This is not a mere grab bag of quick-fix meals for the busy family on the run, even though many of the recipes can be done in no time flat. There is no east meets west, no "Asian pasta," and no garbage. Just great noodle recipes that I have cooked many times over in my long-suffering kitchen. They are recipes with roots; recipes with a tradition and a sense of history that reflect a region, a religion, a way of life, or a season.

Any modern recipes included are still firmly based in the framework of authenticity and have been created by someone who loves, honors, and respects the noodle.

Noodle Survival

There are two ways you can use this book. You can start with a noodle, or you can start with a recipe.

Every noodle type comes with its own noodle ID. Look up the ID to find out what the noodle is, what it looks like, where it comes from, what it's made of, and how to cook it. At the end of every noodle ID is a guide to recipes that use that particular noodle.

So if you find a package of noodles in the cupboard and you don't know what to do with them, simply match them to a picture in the noodle ID and check out the recipes that go with it.

If you already know what you want to cook, then simply look up the recipe, which will tell you the noodle you need. Check the noodle ID before you go shopping, and you'll always cook with the right noodle.

A word on wok-cooking. Always heat your wok first, then add the oil, to prevent food from sticking. When the oil is smoking, add the food. For an authentic flavor, keep your heat up high. It helps to seal the food quickly, as well as imbuing it with the characteristic heat-seared flavor that the Chinese call "the breath of the wok."

As for stir-frying, you don't actually stir. Instead, you toss or flip. Use a paddle or broad spoon to get under the food, flick it up, and toss it over onto itself, rather than stirring. Keep the noodles moving at all times, or they may stick, scorch, or stew. And never put too much in the wok at any one time. Unless you have industrial-strength heat and a giant wok, the noodles will get soggy before they can heat through. If you want to cook for more than four people, buy another wok and run two at once.

It's very, very difficult to undercook a noodle. It's also very, very easy to overcook a noodle. When boiling or soaking your noodles to prepare them for cooking, keep them al dente, so they are still firm to the bite—especially if they are then going into a soup or stir-fry. Above all, trust your instincts. If you want to add more garlic, add more garlic. If you want to leave out the chile, leave out the chile (but you'll go straight to hell when you die). Taste as you go. All you have to do is eat noodles, for long life and happiness.

noodle

1	Wheat noodles
2	Egg noodles
3	Hokkien noodles
4	E-fu noodles
5	Shanghai noodles
6	Sevian
7	Fresh rice sheet noodles
8	Rice vermicelli
9	Fresh round rice noodles
10	Rice sticks
11	Bean thread vermicelli
12	Soba
13	Udon
14	Somen
15	Ramen
16	Harusame
17	Shirataki
18	Naeng myun
19	Dang myun
20	Gooksu

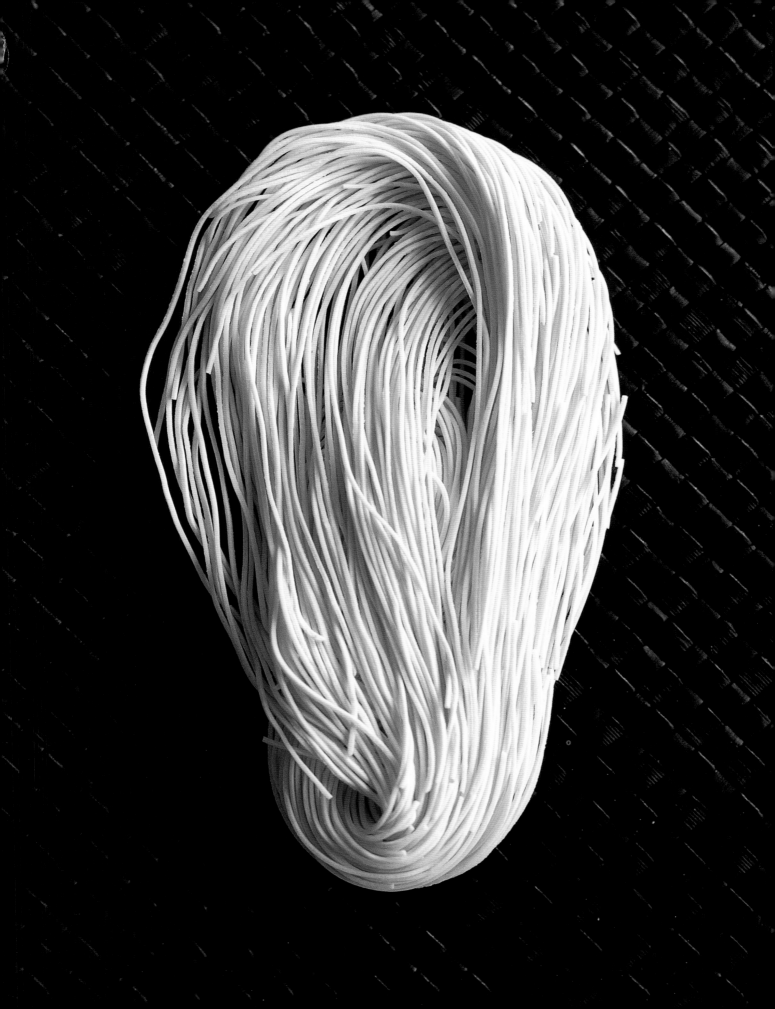

1 Wheat noodles

What	Meet the four-door family sedan of the noodle world. These thin, pale, eggless strands are go-anywhere, do-anything noodles, blessed with an innate toughness and a heart of gold. Available in dried and fresh form, they are usually used dried, even in China. If they had a home, it would be northern China, where most of them end their days in a happy stir-fry. Wheat noodles are also available flavored with shrimp or crab, which sounds like a bad idea. Far better to add your own fresh shrimp or crab.
Why	Because wheat noodles are the noble emperors of the stir-fry. They work with all sorts of textures and flavors, soaking up juices like a sponge, and they're tough enough to withstand domestic abuse.
Where	Burma: *kaukswe*. China: *gan mian* (Mandarin) and *kon mein* (Cantonese). Japan: udon, somen, and ramen are close cousins (see Noodle ID 13, 14, and 15). Korea: *guksoo*. Malaysia: *mee*. Philippines: *miswa*. Thailand: *mee*. Vietnam: *mi soi*.
Which	Look for pale dried noodles sold either in rounds, like mini knitting yarns (shown), or in square blocks. Fresh wheat noodles are sold in plastic bags and should be kept in the refrigerator and used within a week of buying.
How	*Dried*: Cook in plenty of boiling water for about 4 minutes. Rinse in cold water, drain, and reserve until needed. *Fresh*: Cook in plenty of boiling water for about 2 minutes. Rinse in cold water, drain, and reserve until needed.
Whatever	While egg noodles are more giving in texture and a little richer in flavor, they can nevertheless be substituted for wheat noodles. So if you're not sure whether your noodles are wheat or egg, don't worry about it too much. Just keep cooking.
Recipes	Beef and Water Spinach Noodles (page 54); Roast Pork Noodle Soup (page 59); Two-Sides-Brown Noodles with Shredded Duck (page 62); Eight Treasure Noodles (page 85)

2 Egg noodles

What   This is the closest any noodle gets to taking over the world. Seductive, slippery egg noodles stretch from one side of Asia to the other, and joyously cross the boundaries of breakfast, lunch, and dinner. It's the difference between fresh, silken tagliatelle made with eggs, and eggless spaghetti made with tough durum wheat.

Made from wheat flour and egg, they come in various shapes and sizes (see also Noodle ID 3 and 4), but here we want the classic thin, round variety to throw into soups, to stir-fry, and even to deep-fry. If you find thin flat egg noodles, either dried or fresh, save them for soups.

Why   Because they're instant texture food, mouth-filling and bouncy, with a satisfying chew. Because their slipperiness adds a new dimension to even the humblest of their bowling companions. And because they absorb whatever they are given, like an eager student, playing out the flavors of stocks and sauces with every mouthful.

Where   Burma: *kyet-oo kaukswe*. China: *dan mian* (Mandarin) and *dan mein* (Cantonese). Indonesia: *bahmi*. Philippines: *pancit mami*. Thailand and Malaysia: *ba mee*. Vietnam: *mi*.

Which   *Dried*: Look for nestlike bundles of golden noodles (shown), like knitting yarn. Any picture of a hen is a dead giveaway.
Fresh: Check the refrigerated cabinet for plastic bags of sun-tanned golden noodles. These will keep for no longer than a week.

How   *Dried*: Cook in plenty of boiling water for 3 to 4 minutes, or until tender. Drain and rinse under cold running water; drain well. Set aside, covered, until needed.
Fresh: Cook in plenty of boiling water for 1 minute. Drain and rinse under cold running water; drain well. Set aside, covered, until needed. Alternatively, fresh egg noodles can be deep-fried, puffing up into crisp, golden beauties.

Whatever   Don't overcook. You will probably be cooking them again in a stir-fry, braise, or soup, so go for an al dente bounce rather than an "al denture" softness. If precooking, add a little oil to avoid sticking.

Recipes   Eggflower Noodle Soup (page 50); Chiu Chow Dessert Noodles (page 51); Chicken Chow Mein (page 55); Chicken Noodle Soup (page 56); Wonton Soup with Noodles (page 61); Buddhist Vegetable Noodles (page 63); Cold Noodles with Spicy Sichuan Sauce (page 72); Dan Dan Mian (page 73); Sichuan Beef Noodle Soup (page 75); Sichuan Fish Noodles (page 77); Cross the Bridge Noodles (page 78); Dry-Cooked Green Beans with Noodles (page 81); Kao Soi (page 133); Bahmi Goreng (page 171); Panthe Kaukswe (page 175)

3 Hokkien noodles

What Goodbye spaghetti, hello thick, fresh, oiled Hokkien egg noodles. Starring in quick, easy stir-fries all over the globe, they originally started life as a favorite of the Hokkien Chinese, who in turn introduced them to Malaysia, where they play a major role in Malaysian hawker-style dishes, such as *Hokkien mee, mee rebus,* and *mee goreng.*

Why Because of their satisfying, almost meaty bite. By virtue of their size, they take on more sauce and deliver more flavor, so choose Hokkien for all your saucy dishes.

Where Although Hokkien noodles travel the world on a Malaysian passport, they are very big in China, where they are often substituted for the thick white Shanghai noodle. They are also good substitutes for the increasingly rare hand-thrown Peking noodle in many dishes from northern China.

Which Sold fresh or vacuum-packed in plastic bags, in the refrigerated section of Asian food stores and supermarkets. That sunny egg-yolk color, by the way, is probably due more to food dye than sunny egg yolk, so avoid the overly bright ones. Choose loose-packed over vacuum-packed, because they are likely to be fresher, although they won't keep as long.

How Place in a bowl, cover with boiling water, and let stand for about 30 seconds to 1 minute. Drain well, and use for stir-fries and soups.

Whatever Once the preserve of specialty Asian food stores, Hokkien noodles now pop up in suburban supermarkets. However, the noodles available in an Asian store can be superior to the more commercial brands carried by supermarkets.

Recipes Hokkien Noodles with Shrimp (page 67); Sichuan Noodle-Shop Noodles (page 74); Noodles with Pork and Pickles (page 83); Curry Mee (page 116); Hokkien Mee (page 117); Indian Mee Goreng (page 118); Mee Rebus (page 119); Penang Laksa (page 121); Laksa Lemak (page 123); Chile Shrimp Noodles (page 125)

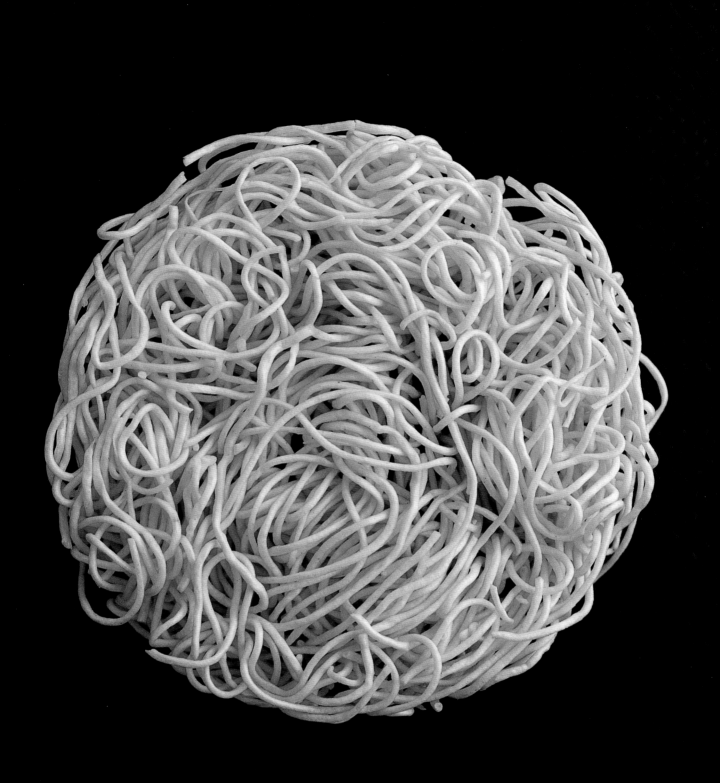

4 E-fu noodles

What	Birthday noodles. These thick, precooked, deep-fried nests of e-fu noodles are a must at birthdays, family celebrations, and Chinese New Year banquets because of their generous length. The longer the noodle you eat, the longer your life will be, and the more good fortune with which you will be blessed—hence the e-fu noodle's alias, long-life noodle.
Why	So you can live longer, of course. Not only that, but every extra meal in your longer life is made more enjoyable by the resilient, sturdy chew that comes from the double-cooking process.
Where	China: *e-fu* (Cantonese) and *shi dan mian* (Mandarin). Philippines: *pancit canton*.
Which	You can't miss 'em. They look like crisp TV snacks that come in large rounds of golden, tangled, swollen noodles, in very large plastic bags. Often, you will find these bags hanging, rather than on a shelf, in your Asian supermarket, as the noodle cakes are quite delicate. Carry home carefully.
How	Weirdly, you need to boil them for 2 or 3 minutes in plenty of water at a rolling boil to soften them, even though they have already been boiled and fried.
Whatever	Don't cut them. That would be seen as deliberately cutting years off the life of the person who eats them, who could be you. The longer, the better.
Recipes	Long-Life Noodles (page 58); Pancit Canton (page 173)

5 Shanghai noodles

What	Big wormlike noodles that are similar to Hokkien noodles, but in a raw state. Shanghai noodles are paler in color and are generally sold fresh, uncooked and unoiled. They are the traditional choice for serving with the famous pork and brown bean sauce the Chinese love as much as the Western world loves spaghetti Bolognese. They are also happy in soups and stir-fries. Shanghai noodles work well in any dish that calls for hand-thrown Peking noodles.
Why	Because they are good, solid, workmanlike noodles that slurp up soups and sauces with a desert island thirst. Because they're a particularly good alternative to the oiled Hokkien noodles when using sauces that are already quite oily.
Where	Northern and eastern China. Naturally, they are very big around Shanghai.
Which	Fresh Shanghai noodles come in plastic bags and are kept in the refrigerated section of Chinese food stores and supermarkets. They are pale, soft, and slightly dusty with flour, and have none of the sheen you see on Hokkien noodles.
How	Boil fresh, raw noodles in plenty of simmering water for about 4 to 5 minutes. Drain and rinse well in cold water, then set aside, covered, until needed.
Whatever	There is also a thin, pale wheat noodle (*mian xian*) that is sometimes referred to as a Shanghai noodle, but most Chinese cookbooks and chefs mean the thicker, more substantial variety when they specify Shanghai noodles.
Recipes	Brown Sauce Noodles (page 49); Stir-Fried Shanghai Noodles (page 70); Gung Bao Chicken with Shanghai Noodles (page 82)

6 Sevian

What	Nobody quite knows how an Italian-style fine vermicelli noodle found its way to India, but nobody is complaining, either. Finer than angel hair pasta, sevian—also called sev—is enjoyed throughout India in a milk pudding known as *sevian kheer*. It is also sometimes used in soups.
Why	Because these noodles have a pleasant fresh bread smell and a good, discernible taste that becomes even more pronounced when fried in ghee (clarified butter). But mainly because of the way they feel in your mouth, brushing it gently like the bristles of a soft shaving brush.
Where	They are a big favorite of Muslim people, so are found in Sri Lanka, Pakistan, and Malaysia, as well as throughout the length and breadth of India itself.
Which	Sevian are always sold dried, normally in protective cardboard boxes, for they are extremely brittle and are hard to handle without causing untold damage. They are usually a pale creamy color, although there is a roasted variety that is a distinctive light brown.
How	Generally, sevian is eaten as *sevian kheer*, and needs only to be boiled in milk along with the other ingredients, for about 15 minutes, so it absorbs some of the milk and flavorings (see recipe, page 181).
Whatever	For an impressive presentation of *sevian kheer*, add fresh rose petals, or a sheet of edible silver or gold leaf, available from specialty food shops, just before serving.
Recipes	Sevian Kheer (page 181)

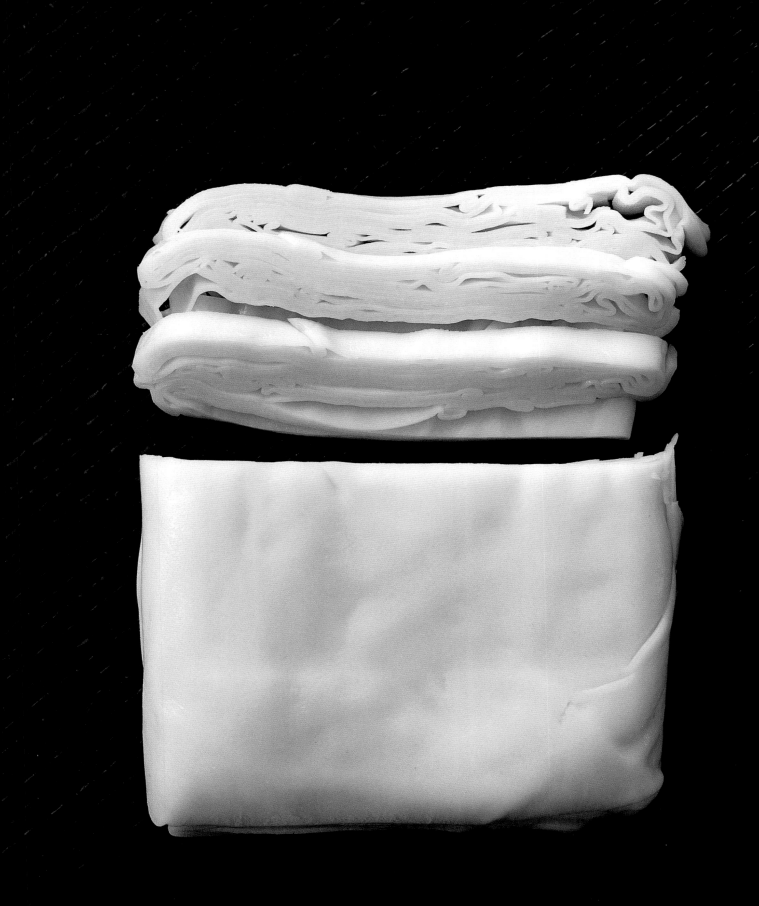

7 Fresh rice sheet noodles

What	These fresh, white, satiny noodles, cut in ribbons from fresh rice sheets, are delivered fresh daily to Asian food stores and supermarkets. Cantonese feast on them wok-tossed with thinly sliced beef, bean sprouts, and soy. Thai people eat them as a lunchtime snack, teamed with beef, curry, pork, or fish balls. Vietnamese devour them for breakfast as *pho bo*, a fragrant soup alive with noodles and beefy bits. Laotians also eat them in soup, flavored with pork, garlic, and a number of herbs, including the leaves of the marijuana plant. Malaysians eat them lightly scorched with the "breath of the wok" in a slippery stir-fry known as as *char kueh teow*.
Why	Because they are so flamboyantly voluptuous, angelically white, and refreshingly fresh, with a silken, slippery quality no dried noodle could ever hope to match.
Where	China: *he fen* (Mandarin) and *hor fun* (Cantonese). Malaysia: *kueh teow*. Thailand and Laos: *sen yai* or *gueyteow*. Vietnam: *pho*. Other: river rice noodles.
Which	Although flat rice noodles are also available in dried form, they really fulfill their silky promise only when fresh. Look for square plastic packages of noodle slabs that look like folded white satin pillowcases. These can then be cut into the desired noodle widths. Precut fresh rice noodles are also widely available.
How	Just slice them into flat noodles of the required width and pour boiling water over to cover. Gently pull the strips apart with a pair of chopsticks, drain, and rinse, and you're ready to toss through a stir-fry or slip into a soup.
Whatever	In spite of the notice on the package to "keep refrigerated," you will probably find them stacked beside, rather than in, the refrigerated cabinet. The truth is they will never taste as good as the day they were made, and while they will indeed keep in the fridge for some time, they will almost instantly lose their generous supple texture and break up when cooked. Fresh is best.
Recipes	Hor Fun Soup Noodles with Roast Duck (page 53); Fried Hor Fun with Beef (page 57); Char Kueh Teow (page 115); Gwaytio Nuea Sap (page 132); Pho Bo (page 152); Pho Ga (page 153)

8 Rice vermicelli

What	The world's most versatile noodles. Throughout Asia, dried rice vermicelli pop up in spring rolls, slither into soups, find their way into a million stir-fries, and puff up dramatically when deep fried. Known as rice stick noodles in China, these thin, dried, brittle white noodles are made from extruded rice flour paste. In southern China, they are often matched with the local seafood.
Why	Because they give texture and contrast to a dish without adding too much bulk. Their neutral, almost bland taste makes them the perfect foil for curries and strongly flavored dishes.
Where	Burma: *hsan kyasan*. China: *mi fen* (Mandarin) and *mai fun* (Cantonese). Malaysia: *beehoon*. Philippines: *pancit bihoon*. Thailand: *sen mee*. Vietnam: *bahn hoi* (an even finer rice vermicelli, used to accompany grilled meat). Other: rice stick noodles (China).
Which	Rice vermicelli are usually sold dried in large bundles wrapped in cellophane. Semitransparent when dried, they turn white when cooked.
How	For use in stir-fries, pour boiling water over to cover and soak for 6 to 7 minutes, or soak in cold water for about 20 minutes. Rinse in cold water and drain. For salads, pour boiling water over to cover for 6 to 7 minutes. Transfer to a saucepan and boil for 1 more minute. For soups, cook noodles directly in plenty of water at a rolling boil for about 2 minutes. Rinse in cold water and drain. To deep-fry, place dried noodles straight into the oil from the packet. They will puff up in much the same manner as shrimp crackers, swelling to roughly four times their original size as if by magic.
Whatever	Don't get lost in the translations. While the Chinese call rice vermicelli "rice sticks," Thai and Vietnamese rice sticks are different again (see Noodle ID 10).
Recipes	Shanghai Pork Noodles (page 69); Chicken Noodle Salad (page 80); Hokkien Mee (page 117); Mee Siam (page 120); Laksa Lemak (page 123); Singapore Beehoon (page 124); Mee Krob (page 131); Moo Sarong (page 135); Thai Chicken Noodle Soup (page 142); Goi Cuon (Fresh Spring Rolls) (page 151); Nem Nuong (page 155); Soto Ayam (page 172); Mohinga (page 174); Stir-Fried Pumpkin with Rice Vermicelli (page 177); Khao Pun Nam Ya (page 178)

9 Fresh round rice noodles

What	Delicate, fresh rice noodles that run from thin varieties, such as the Thai *khanom jeen*, to the thicker type that look like Hokkien noodles without the fake tan. Pale and interesting, they have made their presence felt throughout Southeast Asia, but most particularly in Malaysia, where they perform a public service in the famous *laksa lemak* and *Penang laksa*, and in northern Vietnam, where *bun* noodles feature in a huge range of dishes.
Why	Because this is a truly unique noodle experience, combining the delicate flavor and sublime smoothness of rice vermicelli with the satisfying mouth feel and presence of a thicker noodle.
Where	China: *lai fen*. Malaysia: *laksa*. Philippines: *pancit lug lug*. Thailand: *khanom jeen*. Vietnam: *bun*.
Which	Fresh round rice noodles are generally sold in a variety of thicknesses in plastic-wrapped trays. They will keep at room temperature for two days, or in the fridge for a week, but the quality deteriorates rapidly without refrigeration.
How	Pour boiling water over fresh noodles in a bowl, separating the strands gently, but quickly, with chopsticks, and being careful not to damage the noodles as you go. Drain and refresh in cold water.
Whatever	If you have no luck finding fresh round rice noodles, the thicker variety can be replaced with Hokkien egg noodles (see Noodle ID 3), while the thinner version can be replaced with rice vermicelli or thin rice sticks (see Noodle ID 8 or 10). Dried *khanom jeen* can be found in Thai groceries, but they are a poor substitute for fresh. Malaysian restaurants outside Malaysia often serve both Hokkien noodles and rice vermicelli in their *laksa* soups, instead of the white *laksa* noodle.
Recipes	Penang Laksa (page 121); Laksa Lemak (page 123); Khanom Jeen with Spicy Pork (page 134); Chile Mussels with Rice Noodles (page 140); Thai Chicken Noodle Soup (page 142); Bun Rieu Noodle Soup with Crab Dumplings (page 147); Bun Bo Hué (page 148); Khao Pun Nam Ya (page 178)

10 Rice sticks

What	These dried, translucent noodles act like rice vermicelli that have left home, seen the world, and grown up a bit. They are broader and thicker than rice vermicelli, running from slender sticks to the popular medium-width noodle, resembling pale tagliatelle. Particularly popular in Vietnam, where they are often substituted for fresh rice sheet noodles, and in Thailand, where they are the main attraction of perhaps the most popular Thai noodle dish of all—the mighty *pad Thai*.
Why	Because they are tougher than fresh rice noodles, even after being boiled, and can handle the rough and tumble of the stir-fry, as well as taking it easy in soups. They have more elasticity than fresh rice noodles, which gives them more bounce and bite.
Where	China: *gan he fen* (Mandarin) and *gan hor fun* (Cantonese). Thailand: *sen lek* or *jantaboon*. Vietnam: *hu tieu* or Mekong rice sticks (these also contain tapioca flour).
How	Depending on their size, rice sticks should be boiled for 3 to 5 minutes. Or they can be soaked in warm water for 15 to 20 minutes.
Whatever	Choose your preparation method according to the dish you are cooking. If it is important that the noodles remain rigorously al dente, then soaking is the best method. If you're looking for a more slippery, giving texture, then boiling is the answer.
Recipes	Pad Thai (page 136); Pork and Rice Stick Noodle Soup (page 179)

11 Bean thread vermicelli

What   This noodle has more aliases than the Jackal. Referred to as bean thread, green bean thread, cellophane, jelly, transparent, glass, silver, and even invisible noodles, these thin, opaque white threads are made from an extrusion of mung bean starch and tapioca starch mixed with water. When soaked, they become gelatinous in texture and quite see-through. Their ability to absorb stock makes them ideal for soups, stews, and soupy, braised dishes. They can even be deep-fried, instantly expanding before your very eyes in much the same way as rice vermicelli. They are also popular in desserts, enriched with palm sugar and coconut milk.

Why   Because they wiggle in the mouth, slipping over the tongue with divine lightness; because they look so good (fashionably transparent); and because they're fun to cook with.

Where   Burma: *pekyasan*. China: *fen si* (Mandarin) and *fun see* (Cantonese). Malaysia: *soo hoon* or *tung hoon*. Philippines: *sontanghon*. Thailand: *woon sen*. Vietnam: *bun tau*. Other: Its close cousin, Japan's *harusame* (see Noodle ID 16), is made from rice or potato flour, and Korea's *naeng myun* and *dang myun* (see Noodle ID 18 and 19) are both based on a combination of starches.

Which   Bean thread vermicelli are sold in tight white bundles that resemble rough, wiry, white knitting yarn.

How   Pour boiling water over them in a bowl and let stand for 3 to 4 minutes. Rinse under cold water and drain. If deep-frying, use dry noodles straight from the package.

Whatever   A pair of scissors is a must. These noodles are practically impossible to break by hand when dry and can be quite a handful even after soaking because of their length and propensity to tangle. A few strategic snips here and there will do the trick. When separating the strands for frying, work inside a large plastic or paper bag or you'll find noodles in strange places for months after.

Recipes   Noodles with Shredded Lamb (page 65); Lion's Head Meatballs (page 66); Ants Climbing Trees (page 71); Bang Bang Chicken Noodles (page 79); San Choy Bau with Cellophane Noodles (page 86); Suckling Pig, Jellyfish, and Noodle Salad (page 87); Seafood and Glass Noodle Salad (page 137); Pad Woon Sen (page 139); Glass Noodle Som Tum (page 141); Beef and Glass Noodle Salad (page 143); Cellophane Noodles with Shrimp (page 149); Cha Gio (Finger-Size Spring Rolls) (page 150); Chap Chae (page 159)

12

Soba

What	One of the world's truly great noodle varieties, soba noodles are rugged, tough, protein-rich, and extremely versatile. A lightly flecked, humble mushroom-brown color, they are generally made from a combination of buckwheat and wheat flour, although some exclusively buckwheat flour soba are available. They are usually eaten in soup, or chilled with a dipping sauce. In Tokyo, they represent the very epitome of noodle élan.
Why	Because they taste just as good hot or cold. Because they have a distinctive nutty taste that makes them work even when served on their own with a dipping sauce of dashi, soy, and mirin. And because buckwheat is high in protein, rutin, and vitamins E and C.
Where	Although soba noodles originated in the colder climes of northern Japan, they are equally popular in Tokyo. A distant relative, the *naeng myun* (see Noodle ID 18), is equally revered in Korea, where it is used in much the same way.
Which	Soba are usually sold dried in slim, elegant packages, although some specialty Japanese shops may carry the freshly made variety.
How	*Fresh*: Drop into a pot of boiling water and cook for 2 to 3 minutes, or until al dente. *Dried*: Bring water to a boil, add soba, and when water returns to a boil, add 2 cups of cold water. When water again returns to a boil, add another cup cold water. Repeat the process another 2 to 4 times, depending on the thickness of the soba, until the noodle is cooked but still resilient. Drain, rinse in cold water, and set aside for use.
Whatever	A variation on the theme is the pretty green cha soba, made with the addition of matcha green tea powder. These noodles are more likely to be eaten cold than hot.
Recipes	Zaru Soba (page 101); Tempura Soba (page 103); Soba with Eggplant and Miso (page 110)

13

Udon

What   If the northern soba (see Noodle ID 12) represent Japanese noodle nobility, the udon are the working man's heroes—large, white, country-bumpkin noodles with a simple disposition and a generous nature. Can there be a more satisfying noodle in the world than these fat, glossy beauties? Their spiritual home is in the province of Kagawa on the southernmost island of Shikoku, where official Udon Day is celebrated every year on July 2. Traditionally, these noodles are added to soup, but they can also be served cold and in braised dishes.

Why   Because it's a completely satisfying noodle, with its ample girth and slippery texture. And because the world would be a much poorer place without a bowl of *nabeyaki udon* on a cold winter day.

Where   Udon are generally associated with Osaka and the south of Japan, as opposed to soba, which are generally aligned with Tokyo and the north.

Which   Fresh or fresh/frozen udon noodles are usually bulky, square-cut affairs, while the dried variety can be flat, square, or round. Instant, precooked udon are also sold in small, square shrink-wrapped packages.

How   *Dried*: Place in a pot of boiling water. When water comes back to a boil, add a cup of cold water. When water again comes to a boil, add another cup of cold water. Repeat the process another 2 to 4 times, depending on the thickness of the udon, until the noodle is cooked but still has a little resilience. Drain, rinse in cold water, and set aside.
Fresh: Place in boiling water and cook for 3 to 4 minutes. Drain, rinse in cold water, drain again, and set aside.
Shrink-wrapped instant: Pour boiling water over to cover, and gently separate noodles with a pair of chopsticks. Drain, rinse in cold water, drain again, and set aside.

Whatever   You must slurp your udon noodles. In Japan, slurping noodles of any kind is mandatory, but particularly udon. Because of their generous size and solid nature, they tend to hold the heat longer and are more urgently in need of a cooling intake of air with every slurp.

Recipes   Curry Udon (page 95); Memories of Shikoku Udon (page 97); Fox Noodles with Chicken and Mushrooms (page 98); Nabeyaki Udon (page 99); Odamaki Mushi (page 106); Moon-Viewing Noodles (page 108); Teriyaki Salmon with Udon and Spinach (page 109)

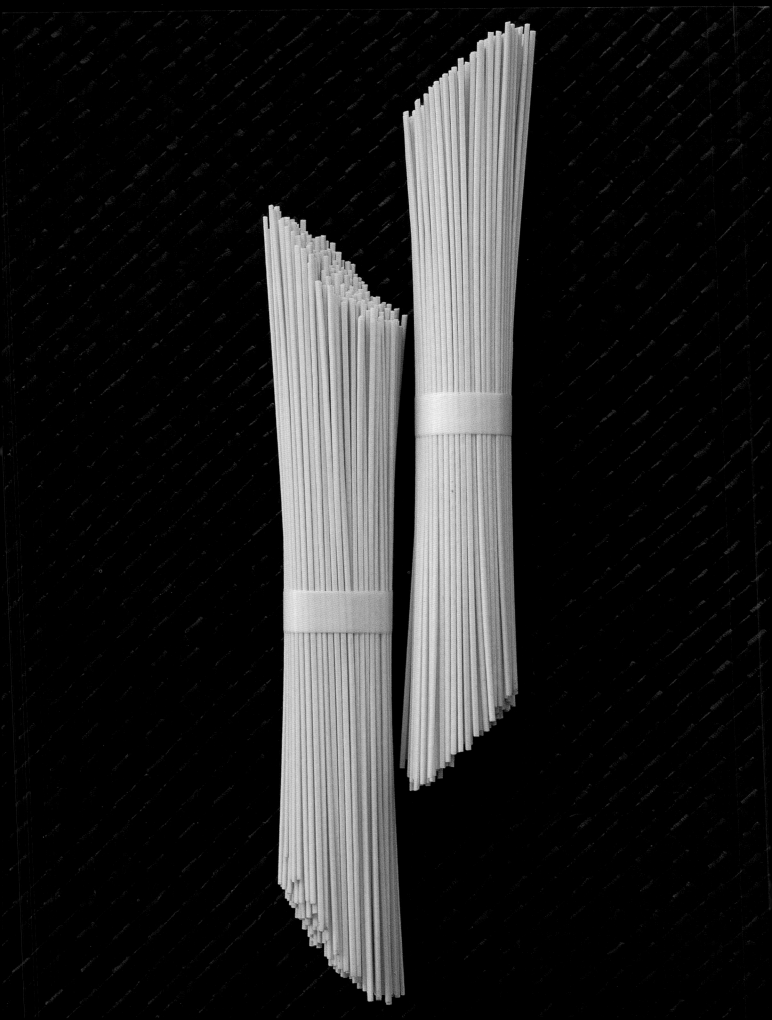

15

Ramen

What	Ramen are not really Japanese, but are based on the Chinese wheat noodle (the name simply means Chinese noodle) and are a popular vending machine and supermarket snack, sold as cup noodles or instant noodles. Japanese noodle purists refuse to recognize them, but there is a noble side to ramen. In Japan, they are also sold by street vendors late at night, and by specialty noodle houses who generally serve the noodles with hot broth, topped with fish cake and pork slices.
Why	For exactly the same reason that wheat noodles are so popular, not only all over Asia, but all over the world. They're no fuss, they're basic, they're recognizable, they're easy, and they make you feel good.
Where	Ramen are popular all over Japan. In western Japan they are more commonly known as *chuka soba*, which are precooked, then dried.
Which	Ramen can be purchased in an instant form, either in a cup or a plastic package, usually with a packet of instant broth. They are also sold dry (shown). Regular Chinese dried egg noodles are a perfect substitute, but fresh, uncooked ramen noodles are best if you're going to cook them in the traditional way in a broth. If you come across a package in your Japanese supermarket labeled *yakisoba*, it does not contain soba noodles but ramen noodles intended for use in stir-fries.
How	*Fresh*: Cook in boiling water for about 2 minutes. Rinse in cold water, drain, and set aside. *Dried*: Cook in boiling water for 3 to 4 minutes. Rinse in cold water, drain, and set aside. *Instant*: Heat according to directions on the package, although you wouldn't find a true noodle lover who would touch an instant noodle with a 10-foot pole.
Whatever	Ramen is the only noodle known to have starred in its own full-length "noodle eastern" feature film, Juzo Itami's *Tampopo*. Get it on video, and learn the way of the noodle.
Recipes	Ramen with Char Sieu (page 107); Five Mushroom Miso with Ramen (page 111)

17

Shirataki

What   Not strictly noodles, shirataki are actually fine strands of *konnyaku*, a jellylike paste made from the root *Amorphophallus konjac,* a Japanese yam known more commonly as devil's tongue plant. This explains shirataki's sinister nickname of "devil's tongue noodles." While they can be added to braised dishes and soups, shirataki are most commonly associated with sukiyaki, a cook-at-the-table dish of beef and vegetables. The name shirataki actually means "white waterfall," due to their shimmering appearance. That is worth creating a haiku while cooking, surely.

Why   Texture, yet again. These "noodles" are all about mouth feel. When combined with another ingredient, they seem to become a part of it, adding a lovely, slippery bounce to something else's flavor.

Where   Japan, but more specifically, the sukiyaki pots of Japan, although similar noodles also turn up in Korea.

Which   Usually shirataki come suspended in water in clear, sausage-shaped plastic packages kept in the fridge at Japanese food stores. They are sometimes also available in cans, which isn't as much fun.

How   Drain the noodles after opening the "sausage" and rinse well under cold water to remove the slightly artificial smell. They are now ready to use.

Whatever   While purists believe that sukiyaki isn't sukiyaki without shirataki, harusame or spring rain noodles (see Noodle ID 16) can be substituted, as can normal bean thread vermicelli (see Noodle ID 11), which are more readily available.

Recipes   Sukiyaki (page 102)

18 Naeng myun

What   The Korean answer to soba, naeng myun are chewier, and paler in appearance. These noodles are usually made from a combination of buckwheat flour and potato starch, although cornstarch is sometimes used. The name translates as "cold noodle," neatly summing up their most popular form of presentation. They are also served hot in soup.

Why   Because the flavor and the texture make them perfect for cold noodle soups, and because the hot Korean summers make it the perfect country for cold noodle soups.

Where   Naeng myun are very much a Korean phenomenon, although Japanese soba noodles can be substituted with great success.

Which   In Korean or Asian grocery stores, naeng myun can occasionally be found fresh/frozen, but the dried variety is easier to find (shown). They have a distinctive, almost plastic, sheen and a pale brown buckwheat color.

How   *Dried*: Put in boiling water for 3 to 4 minutes, or until cooked but still firm. Rinse in cold water, drain, and set aside.
Fresh/frozen: Boil just long enough for them to thaw. Drain and chill until needed.

Whatever   Once cooked, naeng myun can become unwieldy and awkward to handle. A favorite trick of Korean home cooks is to bring a pair of scissors to the table and cut the noodles in each bowl into manageable lengths. Don't cut them too short, however, or you will spoil the fun.

Recipes   Bibim Naeng Myun (page 160); Mul Naeng Myun (page 164)

19 Dang Myun

What	A bigger, tougher, longer, stronger cousin of bean thread vermicelli (see Noodle ID 11), these shimmering, translucent noodles are actually made from sweet potato starch. They require a fair amount of chewing and are popular in soups and stir-fries. Their major role is in Korea's most famous noodle dish, *chap chae*, a stir-fry of noodles, beef, and vegetables.
Why	The beauty of these otherwise drab-looking noodles lies in their resilient, chewy nature and their ability to soak up flavors around them like gastronomic blotting paper.
Where	While transparent noodles are found all over Asia, the dang myun is in a class of its own and is very much a Korean phenomenon, highly sought after by the Korean noodle lover.
Which	These distinctive noodles are grayish in color and are sold dried in 12-inch lengths.
How	Soak in hot water for 10 to 15 minutes to soften. Rinse well in cold water and drain thoroughly. Alternatively, cook in plenty of boiling water for about 3 minutes until they are cooked, but not sloppy. Rinse well in cold water and drain thoroughly. Set aside until needed.
Whatever	Unfortunately, most dang myun noodles imported from Korea, including the popular Assi brand, don't actually call them dang myun on the package because they think we wouldn't know what we were looking for. So look for the words "Korean vermicelli" and check the list of ingredients for "sweet potato starch." Only then can you be sure.
Recipes	Chap Chae (page 159); Mandu Kuk (page 162); Mu Chungol (page 163)

20 Gooksu

What   Gooksu is the generic term for noodle in Korean, although the word usually refers to these long wheat flour noodles. Gooksu, or Korean "knife cut" noodles, were traditionally made at home with wheat flour, egg, and water, and cut into long, thin, pale strips. These days, however, they're more likely to be bought dried, from Korean and Asian food stores. They are generally served in soups and accompanied by spicy kimchee, fermented cabbage. Their most famous incarnation is *kalgooksu*, a spicy, anchovy-flavored soup.

Why   Because it's an earthy, satisfying sort of noodle, one that deserves a good slurp, and good friends to share it with. Or because you're Korean.

Where   Although they bear more than a passing resemblance to udon noodles (but neater and thinner), these noodles are very much a Korean specialty and star attractions of the many noodle shops that make Seoul such a satisfying noodle city.

Which   Dried gooksu noodles are straight, white, and come in both round and flat versions. The round are usually used in soups, while the flat are preferred for stir-fried dishes.

How   Cook dried noodles in plenty of water at a rolling boil for 3 to 4 minutes. The noodles need to remain al dente, so be careful not to overcook. Rinse under cold water and drain thoroughly. Set aside until needed.

Whatever   One former Korean prime minister loved this dish so much that, instead of holding state banquets for visiting diplomats, he would take them home to sample his wife's famous *kalgooksu*.

Recipes   Kalgooksu (page 161)

china

China–Beijing

Brown Sauce Noodles	49
Eggflower Noodle Soup	50

China–Chiu Chow

Chiu Chow Dessert Noodles	51

China–Guangdong

Hor Fun Soup Noodles with Roast Duck	53
Beef and Water Spinach Noodles	54
Chicken Chow Mein	55
Chicken Noodle Soup	56
Fried Hor Fun with Beef	57
Long-Life Noodles	58
Roast Pork Noodle Soup	59
Wonton Soup with Noodles	61
Two-Sides-Brown Noodles with Shredded Duck	62
Buddhist Vegetable Noodles	63

China–Far North

Noodles with Shredded Lamb	65

China–Shanghai

Lion's Head Meatballs	66
Hokkien Noodles with Shrimp	67
Shanghai Pork Noodles	69
Stir-Fried Shanghai Noodles	70

China–Sichuan

Ants Climbing Trees — 71

Cold Noodles with Spicy Sichuan Sauce — 72

Dan Dan Mian — 73

Sichuan Noodle-Shop Noodles — 74

Sichuan Beef Noodle Soup — 75

Sichuan Fish Noodles — 77

China–Yunan

Cross the Bridge Noodles — 78

China–Modern

Bang Bang Chicken Noodles — 79

Chicken Noodle Salad — 80

Dry-Cooked Green Beans with Noodles — 81

Gung Bao Chicken with Shanghai Noodles — 82

Noodles with Pork and Pickles — 83

Eight Treasure Noodles — 85

San Choy Bau with Cellophane Noodles — 86

Suckling Pig, Jellyfish and Noodle Salad — 87

Brown Sauce Noodles (Zha Jiang Mian)

As if there weren't enough arguments over whether it was the Italians or the Chinese who invented noodles (they both did), we are now getting into who invented the Bolognese sauce as well. Here, it is brown bean instead of tomato and pork instead of veal, but we can still feel gratitude for having both in the world.

¼ cup brown bean sauce
½ cup chicken stock
1 tablespoon hoisin sauce
½ teaspoon sugar
2 tablespoons peanut or corn oil
5 green onions, white part chopped, green part of 2 onions thinly sliced
1 tablespoon finely chopped garlic
1 pound ground pork
13 ounces fresh Shanghai noodles
1 cucumber, cut into long matchsticks
1 cup bean sprouts, blanched

Mash brown bean sauce with the back of a spoon and mix well with stock, hoisin sauce, and sugar.

Heat oil in a hot wok and fry the chopped green onions and garlic for 20 seconds. Add pork and stir-fry until it separates into small pieces and is browned, about 2 to 3 minutes. Add the bean mixture, reduce heat, and simmer for 5 minutes.

Cook noodles in boiling water for 4 to 5 minutes. Drain and place in a large bowl. Spoon the brown sauce over them, and arrange a sheaf of cucumber strips on top. Serve with more cucumber strips, sliced green onions, and bean sprouts, so that everyone can help themselves, folding the goodies through the sauce and the noodles.

Serves 4

Eggflower Noodle Soup

This is a serious version of good old chicken and corn soup, but without the chicken and the corn. The trick with the egg is to drizzle it in a very fine stream through the tines of a fork, so that it forms fine threads. Poetic cooks insist the threads look like chrysanthemum petals, but it is perfectly all right if they just look like threads of egg.

10 ounces pork belly or fresh, fatty pork
¼ cup dried wood ear mushrooms, soaked in hot water for an hour
8 dried shiitake mushrooms, soaked in hot water for an hour
2 tablespoons peanut oil
1 tablespoon minced fresh ginger
3 green onions, green part only, thinly sliced
½ cup bamboo shoots, cut into thin strips
4 cups chicken stock
2 tablespoons soy sauce
1 tablespoon shaohsing rice wine or dry sherry
1 teaspoon salt
11 ounces fresh flat wheat noodles
3 ounces cooked ham, cut into thin strips
1 tablespoon cornstarch, mixed with 1 tablespoon cold water
2 eggs, beaten
1 teaspoon sesame oil
½ teaspoon ground pepper

Put pork in a saucepan, cover with cold water, and bring to a boil. Skim off any foam that rises, reduce heat, and simmer for 45 minutes. Turn off the heat and leave pork in the liquid to cool.

Drain the mushrooms and rinse well, then cut into thin strips, discarding the stems.

Cut the cooled pork into thin strips about 1 inch long. Reserve the cooking liquid, skimming off the fat.

Heat peanut oil in a heated saucepan and add ginger, half the green onions, mushrooms, and bamboo shoots and stir-fry briefly. Add chicken stock and 4 cups of the pork cooking liquid and bring to a boil. Add soy sauce, rice wine, and salt, taste, adjust seasonings, and simmer for 3 minutes.

Cook noodles in boiling water for about 1 minute. Drain, rinse in cold water, and drain again.

Add pork and ham to the soup, turn up the heat, and stir in the cornstarch mixture. Stir until the soup thickens, lower heat, and slowly pour the egg into the soup in a thin stream through the tines of a fork. Stir lightly, then add sesame oil and pepper. Divide noodles between 4 bowls. Ladle soup over, and scatter with remaining green onions.

Serves 4

Chiu Chow Dessert Noodles

The Chiu Chow people live near the coast in the province of Guangdong. While their food shares many of the subtleties of the Cantonese, flavors are often punched up with sharp, vinegary dipping sauces. Even their famous dessert noodles are given a good, solid kick along with the addition of a little red vinegar. This wonderfully simple dish is sweet and sour, in its most sublime form.

3 ounces dried egg noodles
2 tablespoons peanut oil
3 tablespoons Chinese red vinegar
3 tablespoons white sugar

Put noodles in a pot of boiling water and simmer for 3 minutes, or until tender. Rinse under cold running water and drain thoroughly. Set aside for 2 hours, then pat dry.

Heat peanut oil in a wok and swirl around to cover the surface. Put noodles in the wok and flatten them against the surface, pressing with the back of a ladle. Cook for about 5 minutes, until golden and crisp on the underside. Place a large plate on top of the wok and invert the wok so that the flat noodle pancake tips out onto the plate. Slide the pancake back in and cook on the other side.

Cut pancake into 4 pieces. Serve with side bowls of red vinegar and sugar. Sprinkle both on top, to your own taste, and eat with chopsticks or fork and spoon.

Serves 4

noodle ID 2

Hor Fun Soup Noodles with Roast Duck

How easy is this? All it takes is a few rice noodles, a ladleful of chicken stock, and a couple of pieces of the Cantonese roast duck you picked up at the Chinese barbecued meat store on the way home. It goes to show that there are times when shopping skills are more important than cooking skills.

2 cloves garlic, crushed with the side of a knife blade
2 slices ginger, cut into thin matchsticks
1 tablespoon oyster sauce
8 cups chicken stock
4 iceberg lettuce leaves
½ Cantonese roast duck (from Chinese barbecued meat store)
10 ounces fresh rice sheet noodles
2 green onions, green part only, sliced

Add garlic, ginger, and oyster sauce to boiling chicken stock and simmer for 5 minutes. Remove garlic. Blanch lettuce leaves quickly in the stock and remove.

Chop duck Chinese-style, through the bone, into 1-inch pieces.

Cut rice sheet noodles into ¾-inch strips and place in a bowl. Pour boiling water over to cover, and quickly but carefully separate the noodles with a pair of chopsticks. Drain and divide among 4 soup bowls. Arrange lettuce leaf on top, and ladle hot soup over the noodles. Put 4 or 5 pieces of duck in each bowl and sprinkle with green onions.

Serves 4

Beef and Water Spinach Noodles

Water spinach, known as ong choy in Cantonese, is a seductive, velvety vegetable that adds a little touch of luxury to anything it comes near. From the subtle crunch of its hollow stems to the intense sweetness of its leaves, it is one of the least boring green vegetables you'll ever meet. Here it turns a homey bowl of beef noodles into something with real depth and character.

7 ounces beef (sirloin or rump steak)
1 tablespoon cornstarch
3 tablespoons soy sauce
1 teaspoon sugar
1 teaspoon shaohsing rice wine or dry sherry
4 tablespoons peanut oil
10 ounces dried wheat noodles
3 ounces water spinach (ong choy), thoroughly washed, dried, and cut into 21/2-inch pieces
2 green onions, thinly sliced
1 tablespoon grated ginger
2 cloves garlic, finely chopped
1 tablespoon hoisin sauce
2 tablespoons chicken stock
½ teaspoon salt
Pinch of black pepper

Finely slice meat into thin matchsticks about 2 inches long. Rub cornstarch into the meat, combine with 1 tablespoon soy sauce, the sugar, rice wine, and 1 tablespoon oil, and leave to marinate for an hour.

Cook noodles in plenty of boiling water for about 4 minutes, or until tender, then rinse well under cold water, drain, and set aside.

Heat 2 tablespoons oil in a hot wok and stir-fry water spinach for a minute or two, moving the spinach continuously. Remove spinach, set aside, and add remaining 1 tablespoon oil to the wok. Stir-fry beef for one minute, add half the green onions, the ginger, garlic, and hoisin sauce and stir-fry for another minute. Add remaining 2 tablespoons soy sauce, stock, salt, and black pepper. When the liquid starts to boil, add the noodles and water spinach and heat through, stirring well to combine. Sprinkle with remaining green onions and serve.

Serves 4

Chicken Chow Mein

Better known as number 42 (or 17, or 91), this would have to be the world's most boring, safe, unadventurous, and uneventful Chinese order ever. Yet somewhere beyond the gloppy cornstarch sauce, the tired, limp vegetables, and that back-of-the-tongue thwack of MSG is something pure, noble, and downright nice that deserves reclaiming.

10 ounces dried egg noodles
7 ounces boneless chicken
5 ounces pork loin
2 tablespoons soy sauce
1 tablespoon shaohsing rice wine or dry sherry
1½ tablespoons cornstarch
2 teaspoons grated ginger
6 dried mushrooms, soaked in hot water for an hour
6 stems choy sum (flowering cabbage)
3 tablespoons peanut oil
4 green onions, cut into 1-inch pieces, plus 2 green onions, green part only, thinly sliced, for garnish
2 teaspoons sesame oil
½ cup chicken stock

Cook noodles in boiling water for 3 to 4 minutes, or until tender. Drain, rinse in cold water, drain again, cover, and set aside.

Cut chicken and pork into thin strips. In large bowl, combine 1 tablespoon soy sauce, rice wine, 1 tablespoon cornstarch, and ginger. Add meat and marinate for 30 minutes.

Cut stems off mushrooms and slice caps into thin strips. Wash choy sum and cut into 2-inch pieces. Put thicker stems in boiling water and cook for a minute. Add thinner stems and leaves and cook for another 30 seconds. Drain and refresh with cold water.

Heat 2 tablespoons peanut oil in a hot wok and stir-fry the meats for 1 minute. Add choy sum, mushrooms, and green onion pieces and cook for 2 minutes. Remove from the wok. Add remaining tablespoon peanut oil to hot wok and stir-fry noodles for about 3 minutes. Return meat and vegetables to wok, along with the sesame oil and remaining 1 tablespoon soy sauce. Toss well. Add chicken stock and remaining ½ tablespoon cornstarch, mixed to a paste with a little cold water (use less cornstarch if the mixture is already starting to thicken). Transfer to a large serving plate and sprinkle with sliced green onions.

Serves 4

noodle ID 2

Chicken Noodle Soup

Forget your packages, cans, pretend noodles, and powdered, super-boosted chicken essences. Real chicken noodle soup is made from real chicken stock, with real chicken pieces and the freshest egg noodles you can lay your hands on. They usually come in a large plastic package and that's the only package you'll ever really need for chicken noodle soup.

1 teaspoon salt
1 egg white, lightly beaten
2 teaspoons cornstarch
2 boneless chicken breasts, cut into thin strips
8 dried shiitake mushrooms, soaked in hot water for an hour
11 ounces fresh flat egg noodles
1 tablespoon peanut oil
3 ounces bamboo shoots, cut into thin matchsticks
½ bunch choy sum (flowering cabbage) leaves, about 7 ounces, coarsely chopped
3 green onions, cut into 1-inch pieces
2 tablespoons light soy sauce
1 tablespoon shaohsing rice wine or dry sherry
1 teaspoon sugar
1 teaspoon sesame oil
8 cups chicken stock, simmering

Combine ½ teaspoon salt, egg white, and cornstarch in a bowl, add chicken, and toss to coat. Leave for 20 minutes to "velvet" the chicken. Drain mushrooms, remove stems, and thinly slice caps.

Cook noodles in boiling water for 2 minutes, rinse in cold water, and drain well.

Heat oil in a hot wok and stir-fry chicken, bamboo shoots, and mushrooms for 2 minutes. Add choy sum and green onions and stir-fry for another minute. Add soy sauce, rice wine, sugar, sesame oil, and remaining ½ teaspoon salt.

Add noodles to the stock and bring to a boil. Add the contents of the wok, stir through, and serve in Chinese bowls with soup spoons and chopsticks.

Serves 4

noodle ID 2

Fried Hor Fun with Beef

The Cantonese consider the feel or texture of food to be just as important, if not more important, than the flavor. Here, the overriding quality is slipperiness. The beef is marinated with cornstarch to give it a smooth, silky feel, while the already slinky rice noodles are made even slinkier by mixing them with the "cooked-oil" sauce. The end result feels like a delicious, edible slippery dip.

1 pound fresh rice sheet noodles
¼ cup plus 1 teaspoon peanut oil
7 ounces lean beef, thinly sliced
2 tablespoons plus 1 teaspoon light soy sauce
1 teaspoon cornstarch, mixed with 1 tablespoon cold water
2 tablespoons dark soy sauce
1 teaspoon sugar
2 slices ginger, cut into thin matchsticks
2 green onions, finely chopped
1 cup bean sprouts, rinsed

Cut rice sheets into ¾-inch strips, if not already cut. Place in a bowl and pour boiling water over to cover, gently shaking strips apart with a pair of chopsticks. Immediately drain and cool under cold running water. Drain well and mix with 1 teaspoon peanut oil to prevent sticking.

Heat remaining ¼ cup peanut oil in a hot wok, cook for 2 minutes, then cool. Mix 2 tablespoons of this cooked oil with beef, 1 teaspoon light soy sauce, and cornstarch mixture, and marinate for 30 minutes. Mix dark soy sauce, remaining light soy sauce, and sugar and set aside.

Heat remaining 2 tablespoons cooked oil in a hot wok and cook ginger and green onions for 1 minute, then remove. Add beef mixture and stir-fry for 1 minute until it changes color. Remove beef and set aside. Add bean sprouts to wok and stir-fry for 1 minute. Lift out and set aside. Add drained noodles and stir-fry for 2 minutes. Add soy sauce mixture and stir well. Return beef to the wok and stir, mixing thoroughly. Serve on a large platter or in small Chinese bowls.

Serves 4

noodle ID 7

Long-Life Noodles

No celebration or banquet is complete without a dish of long-life noodles, served either at the very beginning or the very end. The idea is simple: the longer the noodle, the longer you will live. And of course, the longer you live, the more long-life noodles you will get to eat. There is something rather endearing about Chinese logic.

4 green onions
8 dried shiitake mushrooms, soaked in hot water for an hour
1 large e-fu noodle cake, about 11 ounces
¾ cup chicken stock
2 tablespoons soy sauce
1 tablespoon oyster sauce
1 teaspoon sesame oil
1 teaspoon sugar
1 tablespoon peanut oil
1 tablespoon grated ginger
2 cloves garlic, crushed with the side of a knife blade

Thinly slice the green tops of the green onions and reserve. Cut the remainder into very thin matchsticks. Drain mushrooms, discard stems, and thinly slice caps.

Cook noodles in boiling water for 3 to 4 minutes. Rinse in cold water and drain well.

Mix chicken stock, soy sauce, oyster sauce, sesame oil, and sugar in a bowl and set aside.

Heat peanut oil in a hot wok and stir-fry ginger and garlic for 1 minute. Add green onion matchsticks, all of the mushrooms, and sauce ingredients and bring to a boil, stirring. Cook for 1 minute. Add noodles and cook for about 2 minutes, or until they have absorbed most of the sauce. Serve immediately, scattered with remaining green onions.

Serves 4

noodle ID 4

Roast Pork Noodle Soup

No self-respecting noodle lover should ever live more than a short drive from a Chinese barbecued meat shop. Of course, you can make your own char sieu (see Basics, page 189) and keep it in the fridge, but that way, you can't pick up a piece of suckling pig and a little white cut chicken at the same time.

7 ounces dried wheat noodles
½ bunch gai laan (Chinese broccoli), about 11 ounces
3 tablespoons peanut oil
6 slices ginger, cut into matchsticks
2 tablespoons soy sauce
2 tablespoons oyster sauce
1 tablespoon shaohsing rice wine or dry sherry
1 tablespoon cornstarch, mixed with a little cold water
2 teaspoons sugar
2 teaspoons sesame oil
½ teaspoon salt
Pinch of black pepper
7 ounces char sieu (red roast pork), cut into thin slices
2 green onions, cut on the diagonal into 1-inch pieces, plus 1 green onion, green part only, cut into 1-inch pieces, for garnish
8 cups chicken stock

Cook noodles in plenty of boiling water for 4 minutes, or until tender, then rinse well under cold water, drain, and set aside.

Cut gai laan into 2½-inch pieces. Put thick stems in a pot of boiling water and cook for 1 minute. Add leaves and thinner stems and cook for 20 seconds. Remove from pot and plunge into cold water. When cool, drain and set aside.

Heat peanut oil in a hot wok and stir-fry ginger for 1 minute. Add gai laan and stir-fry for another minute. Add soy sauce, oyster sauce, rice wine, cornstarch mixture, sugar, sesame oil, salt, and pepper. Bring liquid just to a boil, add pork and green onions, and heat through, stirring.

In a separate pot, bring chicken stock to a boil. Put noodles in a strainer or colander and pour boiling water over to warm them. Drain well. To serve, put a handful of noodles into each of 4 bowls. Pour chicken stock over noodles and top with pork mixture. Scatter remaining green onion on top and serve with spoons and chopsticks.

Serves 4

Wonton Soup with Noodles

If there were one dish that summed up everything that was good, pure, and nourishing about Cantonese food, this would be it. It is subtle, gentle, fragrant, thoroughly clean tasting, and almost a monument to the freshness and quality of the ingredients that go into its making. The Chinese eat it for a full-on breakfast, a fast lunch, a satisfying supper, and sometimes for a homey, easy dinner. In other words, all the time.

5 ounces shrimp, peeled, deveined, and finely minced
5 ounces ground pork
2 tablespoons pork or bacon fat, finely minced
4 dried shiitake mushrooms, soaked in hot water for an hour, drained, stemmed, and
   finely minced
4 water chestnuts, finely chopped
2 green onions, white part finely chopped, green part sliced for garnish
1 small egg white
Salt and pepper to taste
8 ounces fresh egg noodles
1 package fresh wonton wrappers (approximately 20 wrappers)
1 teaspoon cornstarch mixed with 1 tablespoon cold water
8 cups chicken stock
2 slices ginger, peeled
3 ounces choy sum (flowering cabbage), washed and thickly sliced

To make dumpling mixture, combine shrimp, pork, pork fat, mushrooms, water chestnuts, chopped green onions, egg white, salt, and pepper in a bowl and mix with your hands until thoroughly blended. Refrigerate for 1 hour.

Cook noodles in boiling water for 1 to 2 minutes. Drain, rinse with cold water, drain again, and set aside.

Lay a wonton wrapper on the work surface. Put a teaspoon of filling in the center. Dip your finger in the cornstarch paste and run it around the edges. Fold over to form a triangle, pressing the edges together. Bring the 2 extreme corners together to meet and overlap in the middle, and seal with a little paste. Repeat until all filling is used (about 20 wontons).

Heat stock in a saucepan, add ginger, and bring to a simmer. Blanch choy sum in boiling water for 1 minute, drain, and add to stock. Drop dumplings in a pot of boiling water and cook until they float to the surface, about 4 to 5 minutes. Drain and distribute among 4 deep warmed soup bowls. Pour boiling water over noodles in a strainer over the sink to warm. Drain and divide among the bowls. Discard ginger and pour stock on top. Scatter with sliced green onions.

Serves 4

noodle ID 2

Two-Sides-Brown Noodles with Shredded Duck

It may seem something of a pointless exercise, creating a crisp, crunchy noodle pancake just so you can pour sauce all over it, and make the noodles go soggy again. But that is exactly the point. If you don't get it now, you will with your first mouthful.

7 ounces dried wheat noodles (thin)
6 dried shiitake mushrooms, soaked in water for an hour
4 tablespoons peanut oil
2 cloves garlic, crushed with the side of a knife blade
2 slices ginger
1 bunch choy sum (flowering cabbage), cut into 2-inch sections
3 ounces bamboo shoots, cut into matchsticks
8 water chestnuts, thinly sliced
1 lup cheong sausage, cut into matchsticks
Meat from ½ Chinese roast duck, thinly sliced
1 cup bean sprouts, rinsed
½ cup chicken stock
1 tablespoon oyster sauce
1 tablespoon soy sauce
1 teaspoon cornstarch
1 tablespoon shaohsing rice wine or dry sherry
3 green onions, thinly sliced

Drop noodles into a pot of boiling water and cook for about 4 minutes. Rinse under cold water and drain well. Drain mushrooms, remove stems, and thinly slice caps.

Heat 2 tablespoons peanut oil in a hot wok and cook 1 clove of garlic and 1 slice of ginger for a minute to flavor the oil, then remove. Add thicker choy sum stems and stir-fry for 2 minutes. Add mushrooms, bamboo shoots, water chestnuts, lup cheong, and duck and stir-fry for 2 minutes. Add choy sum leaves and bean sprouts and stir-fry until they soften. Add stock, oyster sauce, and soy sauce and toss lightly. Mix cornstarch with rice wine and stir into the mixture. Tip everything into a heatproof bowl and keep warm in a low oven.

Heat remaining 2 tablespoons peanut oil in a hot wok and cook remaining ginger and garlic for 1 minute until golden, then discard. Tip noodles into wok and flatten them against the surface. Cook for 4 to 5 minutes, until golden brown. Place a flat plate on top of the wok and invert the whole thing so noodle pancake falls onto the plate. Return wok to heat, add a little extra oil, slide pancake back in, and cook the other side. Turn out on a large, warmed serving platter and top with stir-fried mixture and green onions.

Serves 4

noodle ID 1

Buddhist Vegetable Noodles

In China, Buddhist monks go to extreme lengths to create vegetarian food that looks, smells, and even tastes like fish or meat. For me, however, the most successful vegetable dishes in the Chinese repertoire are those that look like vegetables. This is based on a classic Buddhist vegetarian dish that manages to satisfy both aesthetically and gastronomically.

3 tablespoons peanut oil, plus 1 teaspoon extra for tossing
1 small onion, sliced lengthwise
2 cloves garlic, finely chopped
2 slices ginger, finely chopped
8 dried shiitake mushrooms, soaked in hot water for 1 hour and sliced (reserve soaking water)
1 tablespoon vegetarian oyster sauce (yes, it does exist, see Glossary, page 196)
3 tablespoons light soy sauce
2 cups shredded Tientsin cabbage
½ red bell pepper, thinly sliced
½ green bell pepper, thinly sliced
3 tablespoons bamboo shoots, cut into matchsticks
½ medium carrot, thinly sliced
1 cup bean sprouts, rinsed
½ teaspoon sugar
½ teaspoon salt
Pinch of white pepper
1 tablespoon shaohsing rice wine, or dry sherry
2 teaspoons sesame oil
10 ounces fresh Chinese egg noodles
2 green onions, green part only, thinly sliced

Heat 1 tablespoon peanut oil in a hot wok and stir-fry onion until translucent. Add garlic, ginger, and mushrooms and cook for another minute. Add oyster sauce and 2 tablespoons soy sauce and cook for another 30 seconds. Transfer wok contents to a bowl. Heat 2 tablespoons peanut oil in the hot wok and stir-fry cabbage, bell peppers, bamboo shoots, and carrot for 3 minutes. Add bean sprouts, sugar, ¼ cup reserved mushroom water, salt, and pepper and cook for 1 minute. Add onion and mushroom mixture, rice wine, and sesame oil and combine well.

Cook noodles in plenty of water at a rolling boil for about a minute. Drain thoroughly, rinse under cold running water, and drain well. Toss with remaining 1 tablespoon soy sauce and remaining 1 teaspoon peanut oil. Put noodles on a large warmed serving platter, spoon vegetable mixture over, and mix lightly. Sprinkle with green onions and serve.

Serves 4

noodle ID 2

Noodles with Shredded Lamb

In the cooking of the south of China, lamb is very unusual, and the Cantonese, not great fans of its smell or taste, are easily able to distinguish "mutton-eaters" by their smell. But up north, lamb means survival, and the meat features in countless regional specialties. This simple dish combines lamb and noodles in an easy, ingenious way that even a Cantonese could learn to love.

7 ounces bean thread vermicelli
7 ounces lean, boneless lamb fillet (such as sirloin or leg steak)
1 egg, beaten
2 tablespoons water
1 tablespoon cornstarch
½ teaspoon salt
2 tablespoons peanut oil
3 tablespoons soy sauce
3 green onions, green part only, cut into 2-inch pieces
1 cup chicken stock
2 tablespoons shaohsing rice wine or dry sherry
1 teaspoon sesame oil

Put noodles in a bowl, pour boiling water over, and let soak for 3 to 4 minutes. Rinse in cold water, drain, and set aside.

Cut lamb into thin strips. Combine the beaten egg, water, cornstarch, and salt in a bowl. Add lamb and coat well in the mixture and set aside for 10 to 15 minutes. Heat peanut oil in a hot wok and stir-fry lamb for 1 to 2 minutes. Add soy sauce and green onions and stir-fry for another minute. Add chicken stock, noodles, rice wine, and sesame oil and cook for another 2 minutes. Serve on a large warmed platter or in Chinese bowls.

Serves 4

noodle ID 11

Lion's Head Meatballs

The extremely romantic name suggests that these giant, moist meatballs, when surrounded by a "mane" of cabbage and noodles, look just like lions' heads. Yeah, right. The soft, light, almost moussey meatballs are traditionally made by repeatedly bashing the meat against the side of the bowl to break down its structure, but you can purée it in the food processor instead for a similar result. A hint: for Chinese cooking, ground pork from an Asian butcher is always preferable to that from a non-Asian butcher.

6 dried shiitake mushrooms
3 ounces bean thread vermicelli
1¼ pounds ground pork
1 egg white
3 green onions, chopped
2 slices ginger, finely chopped
1 tablespoon cornstarch plus extra for rolling meatballs
1 tablespoon shaohsing rice wine or dry sherry
Salt to taste
2 tablespoons peanut oil
3 cups chicken stock, heated
2 tablespoons soy sauce
4 baby bok choy (Chinese cabbage)

Pour boiling water over mushrooms and let soak for about an hour. When soaked, lightly squeeze dry and discard the stems. Pour boiling water over the noodles and leave for 3 to 4 minutes to soften. Rinse in cold water, drain, and set aside until needed.

Put pork, egg white, green onions, ginger, cornstarch, rice wine, and salt in a food processor and blend until smooth. With your hands, shape the mixture into large meatballs about 2 inches in diameter. Roll meatballs in a little extra cornstarch. Heat oil and fry meatballs until lightly golden.

Add chicken stock, mushrooms, and soy sauce to meatballs in a clay pot or large saucepan and bring to a boil. Cover, reduce heat, and cook gently for 45 minutes.

Clean bok choy, cut in half lengthwise, and add with noodles to the pot. Cook for another 10 minutes. Bring the pot to the table to serve or spoon into Chinese bowls.

Serves 4

noodle ID 11

Hokkien Noodles with Shrimp

Please try to put any passing resemblance between this and combination chow mein out of your mind. This is an intriguing, "soft" combination of flavor and texture, lit up by the surprising, gentle Shanghainese sweetness that comes from the sugar and the ketchup.

1 pound Hokkien noodles
7 ounces small shrimp, peeled and deveined
Pinch of salt, plus more to taste
3 teaspoons cornstarch
7 ounces pork loin
3 tablespoons soy sauce
4 tablespoons peanut oil
2 small onions (or 4 shallots), thinly sliced
¾ cup chicken stock
1 tablespoon ketchup
1 tablespoon sugar
1 teaspoon sesame oil

Put noodles in a heatproof bowl, cover with boiling water, and let soak for 1 minute. Drain well and set aside. Mix shrimp with a pinch of salt and 1 teaspoon cornstarch. Cut pork into thin strips and mix with 1 tablespoon soy sauce and 1 teaspoon cornstarch and let stand for 20 minutes.

Heat 2 tablespoons peanut oil in a hot wok and stir-fry shrimp for 1 minute. Remove from wok. Add another tablespoon oil and stir-fry pork for about 2 minutes. Remove from wok. Add 1 tablespoon of oil and cook onions until soft. Add 2 tablespoons soy sauce, the stock, ketchup, sugar, sesame oil, and salt to taste.

Bring to a boil, add noodles, and cook for 1 to 2 minutes. Return pork and shrimp to the hot wok and toss well. Mix remaining teaspoon cornstarch with a teaspoon of cold water and stir through sauce until it thickens slightly. Serve on a warm platter or in small Chinese bowls.

Serves 4

noodle ID 3

Shanghai Pork Noodles

I tried to make this dish more difficult. I tried to make the recipe longer. I tried to make it complicated and confusing. But no matter what I did, it still worked out to be one of the simplest, fastest, and most foolproof dishes in the whole book. Essentially, it's a Cantonese stir-fry, with a bit of added interest.

4 dried shiitake mushrooms, soaked in hot water for an hour
2 tablespoons dried shrimp
10 ounces rice vermicelli
2½ ounces pork loin
1 small leek, trimmed
2 tablespoons peanut oil
1 stalk celery, finely chopped
2 ounces bamboo shoots, cut into matchsticks
½ cup chicken stock
2 tablespoons soy sauce
1 teaspoon salt
1 teaspoon sugar

Drain mushrooms, cut off and discard stems, and thinly slice caps. Soak dried shrimp in warm water for 30 minutes, then drain. Pour boiling water over noodles and let soak for 6 to 7 minutes, until tender. Drain and set aside until needed. Cut pork and leek into matchstick strips.

Heat oil in a hot wok and stir-fry pork for 1 minute. Add shrimp, celery, bamboo shoots, and leek, and stir-fry for 1 minute. Add noodles and toss through. Add stock, soy sauce, salt, and sugar, and cook until liquid has been absorbed by the noodles.

Serves 4

noodle ID 8

Stir-Fried Shanghai Noodles

A simple stir-fry technique produces a surprisingly complex and many-layered dish, underlaid by the gorgeously silky quality of the Shanghai noodles. You can use any kind of Chinese cabbage, but the even, uniform crunch of the white Tientsin, or Peking cabbage, makes it a natural.

13 ounces Shanghai noodles
1 teaspoon sesame oil
3 ounces lean pork
3 ounces boneless chicken thigh meat
3 tablespoons peanut oil
11 ounces Tientsin cabbage, finely shredded
1 stalk celery, finely diced
1 cup chicken stock
3 tablespoons dark soy sauce
¼ teaspoon white pepper

Boil noodles in plenty of simmering water for 4 to 5 minutes. Drain, rinse in cold water, and drain again. Toss with sesame oil and set aside until needed.

Cut pork and chicken into matchsticks. Heat peanut oil in a hot wok and stir-fry meats for 1 minute. Add cabbage and celery and stir-fry for 2 minutes. Add noodles and stir-fry for another minute. Add stock, dark soy sauce, and white pepper and stir-fry until liquid has been absorbed by the noodles. Serve on a warm platter or in small Chinese bowls.

Serves 4

Ants Climbing Trees

A Chinese chef once told me that when a Chinese diner drops a glass at a banquet, that person would never say, "Oops, I dropped a glass." Instead, they would say, "It falls like an opening blossom, rich and noble." The Sichuanese have an equally poetic way with food. This dish can actually look like ants climbing trees, especially if you drink enough mui kwe lu *rosé wine.*

8 ounces ground pork
2 tablespoons light soy sauce
1 tablespoon sugar
1 tablespoon chile bean sauce
1 teaspoon cornstarch
7 ounces bean thread vermicelli
3 tablespoons peanut oil
1 green onion, finely chopped, plus 1 green onion, green part only, thinly sliced, for garnish
1 small red chile, finely chopped
½ cup chicken stock
1 tablespoon dark soy sauce

Combine pork, light soy sauce, sugar, chile bean paste, and cornstarch and let stand for 20 minutes.

Pour boiling water over noodles in a bowl and let stand for 3 to 4 minutes, until tender. Drain.

Heat oil in a hot wok and cook chopped green onion and chile for about 30 seconds. Add pork mixture and stir-fry for 2 to 3 minutes, then add noodles and mix well.

Add chicken stock and dark soy sauce and bring to a boil. Cook for a few more minutes until the liquid has all but disappeared into the noodles. Scatter with sliced green onion and serve.

Serves 4

noodle ID 11

Cold Noodles with Spicy Sichuan Sauce

Beware, these cold noodles are hot, if you get my drift. Underscored by the fire of chile bean sauce and the stinging tickle of Sichuan pickle, this is pure Sichuan pleasure in a bowl.

1 chicken, about 2½ pounds, cooked
13 ounces fresh egg noodles
2 teaspoons sesame oil
3 tablespoons peanut oil
2 tablespoons light soy sauce
2 tablespoons minced Sichuan preserved vegetable
1 tablespoon Sichuan chile bean sauce
1 green onion, thinly sliced
1 teaspoon sugar
½ teaspoon salt
1 tablespoon roasted sesame seeds
½ cucumber, cut into fine matchsticks

Remove meat from chicken and shred into strips.

Put noodles in a pot of boiling water and cook for 1 to 2 minutes. Drain and rinse in cold water. Drain again, being careful to shake off all excess water. Toss noodles in sesame oil to prevent them from sticking and set aside to cool.

Heat peanut oil in a small saucepan until it is almost smoking. Remove from heat and add soy sauce, preserved vegetable, chile bean sauce, green onion, sugar, and salt, stirring well. Leave to cool for about 20 minutes. Combine sauce with noodles, sesame seeds, cucumber, and chicken.

Serves 4

Dan Dan Mian

The name of this dish translates as "pole carrying noodles," referring to the shoulder poles that noodle sellers used to carry their edible wares. These days, the good people of Sichuan are more likely to eat this distinctively different, sweet, spicy, nutty dish in specialty dan dan noodle shops. It's hard to say who is going to like this dish more: noodle freaks or peanut butter addicts.

1 teaspoon peanut oil
1 tablespoon grated ginger
2 teaspoons sugar
1 cup bean sprouts
1 tablespoon sesame seeds
3 tablespoons Chinese sesame paste or peanut butter
2 tablespoons chicken stock
2 teaspoons red chile oil
1 teaspoon sesame oil
1 tablespoon light soy sauce
1 tablespoon Chinese black vinegar
½ teaspoon Sichuan pepper or black pepper, ground
13 ounces fresh egg noodles
2 green onions, finely chopped

Mix peanut oil with grated ginger and sugar. Blanch bean sprouts in a pot of boiling water for 30 seconds, drain, rinse, and set aside.

Toast sesame seeds in a dry pan just until they start to turn brown. Crush lightly.

Mix the oil and ginger mixture with sesame paste, stock, chile oil, sesame oil, and toasted sesame seeds until well blended. Add soy sauce, vinegar, and pepper.

Cook noodles in plenty of boiling water for about 1 minute. Rinse, drain, and arrange on a large platter. Pour sauce over the top and scatter with bean sprouts and green onions.

Serves 4

noodle ID 2

Sichuan Noodle-Shop Noodles

A favorite street-food dish from the noble province of Sichuan, and a great party dish. To turn it into something special, all you need is a pile of disposable chopsticks and a stack of Chinese take-out boxes for fun serving bowls that you won't have to wash later.

6 dried shiitake mushrooms, soaked in hot water for an hour
1 pound Hokkien noodles
2 tablespoons peanut oil
12 fresh straw mushrooms or button mushrooms, thinly sliced
6 tablespoons slivered bamboo shoots
1 teaspoon Sichuan chile oil
2 tablespoons dried shrimp, soaked in hot water for 30 minutes
2 tablespoons light soy sauce
1 tablespoon shaohsing rice wine or dry sherry
1 teaspoon ground Sichuan peppercorns
2 green onions, green part only, thinly sliced

Drain shiitake mushrooms, remove stems, and cut caps in half. Pour boiling water over noodles in a large bowl and let stand for 1 minute. Drain.

Heat peanut oil in a hot wok and cook shiitake and straw mushrooms, bamboo shoots, noodles, and chile oil for 2 to 3 minutes. Add drained shrimp, soy sauce, rice wine, and peppercorns and cook for 1 minute. Serve on a large warmed platter or in Chinese bowls, scattered with green onions.

Serves 4

Sichuan Beef Noodle Soup

This is not the world's daintiest, most elegant soup. It's meaty, chunky, spicy, with an in-your-face belt of chile that lingers in the mouth like a sultry, warm wind. When you've had a bowl of this, you really know you've eaten.

1 pound stewing beef
2 tablespoons peanut oil
4 slices ginger, cut into matchsticks
3 cloves garlic, finely chopped
6 cups water
4 cups chicken stock
2 tablespoons chile bean sauce
2 tablespoons shaohsing rice wine or dry sherry
2 tablespoons dark soy sauce
1 tablespoon sugar
1 star anise
13 ounces fresh egg noodles
1 green onion, finely chopped
1 teaspoon sesame oil
White pepper to taste

Cut beef into pieces about 1 inch square.

In a large saucepan, heat peanut oil and stir-fry ginger and garlic for 20 seconds, then add beef and stir-fry for 2 to 3 minutes. Add water, stock, chile bean sauce, rice wine, soy sauce, sugar, and star anise, and cover. Gently simmer for 2½ hours, until beef is tender.

Cook noodles in boiling water for about a minute. Drain, then divide among 4 large soup bowls. Ladle some beef and soupy sauce over the top. Add green onion, a drizzle of sesame oil, and white pepper.

Serves 4

noodle ID 2

Sichuan Fish Noodles

Being totally landlocked, Sichuan hasn't produced a lot of fish recipes, and the few that exist usually call for freshwater fish. But this dish works swimmingly with ocean fish, especially deep-flavored, firm-fleshed fish. Be warned, the chile bean sauce is pretty fiery stuff.

8 ounces firm white-fleshed fish fillets
2 tablespoons shaohsing rice wine or dry sherry
1 egg white
2 teaspoons cornstarch
3 tablespoons peanut oil
3 ounces water chestnuts, finely chopped
2 ounces bamboo shoots, cut into thin matchsticks
2 green onions, green part only, thinly sliced
1 tablespoon grated ginger
1 clove garlic, finely chopped
1 cup chicken stock
1 tablespoon chile bean sauce
1 tablespoon dark soy sauce
13 ounces fresh egg noodles

Cut fish into small bite-size pieces and mix with 1 tablespoon rice wine, egg white, and cornstarch. Heat 2 tablespoons oil in a hot wok and stir-fry fish for 1 minute. Pour in any remaining marinade and remaining tablespoon rice wine. Add water chestnuts and bamboo shoots and stir-fry for another 30 seconds.

Remove the fish mixture, give the wok a quick wipe, then heat the remaining 1 tablespoon oil and stir-fry green onions, ginger, and garlic for 20 seconds. Add chicken stock, chile bean sauce, and soy sauce. Cook, stirring, for 1 minute, then return fish mixture to the wok. Stir well.

Meanwhile, cook egg noodles in a pot of boiling water for 1 minute. Drain well, add noodles to the wok, and toss well to heat through. Serve on a warmed serving platter or in Chinese bowls.

Serves 4

noodle ID 2

Cross the Bridge Noodles

In this updated version of the Yunan classic, I have dispensed with the layer of chicken fat on top (see Crossing the Bridge, page 182), and instead, I briefly heat everything on the stove in a serving pot and serve the soupy noodles at the table. Another way would be to place the pot on a portable gas table stove and put everything into the pot while the stock is boiling, then turn off the heat. If, of course, you are taking it to an errant scholar, put the layer of chicken fat on top.

10 ounces fresh egg noodles
7 ounces large shrimp, peeled and deveined
1 boneless chicken breast, skinned
7 ounces white fish fillet
½ bunch choy sum (flowering cabbage)
8 cups chicken stock
1 teaspoon finely chopped ginger
1 teaspoon shaohsing rice wine or dry sherry
1 teaspoon soy sauce
1 teaspoon salt
1 teaspoon sugar

Cook noodles in plenty of boiling water for 1 minute. Drain and rinse under cold running water; drain well. Set aside, covered, until needed.

Thinly slice shrimp on the diagonal. Thinly slice chicken breast and fish fillet on the diagonal. Blanch choy sum stems and leaves for 1 minute in simmering water, drain, refresh in cold water, drain again, and set aside.

Heat chicken stock in a large clay pot or a flameproof casserole dish attractive enough to take to the table. Add ginger, rice wine, soy sauce, salt, and sugar and bring to a boil. Add the chicken and fish, and simmer for 4 to 5 minutes, skimming if necessary. Add noodles, shrimp, and choy sum and heat through. Remove from the heat, bring to the table, and serve in small Chinese bowls.

Serves 4

noodle ID 2

Bang Bang Chicken Noodles

Traditionally, this popular dish from northern China—of poached chicken in a nutty, sweet, chile sauce—doesn't include noodles. Yet the subtle crunch of the bean thread vermicelli adds substance and character, and lightens a meat-heavy dish. I think it's an improvement.

7 ounces bean thread vermicelli
2 teaspoons sesame oil
1 chicken, about 2½ pounds
2 green onions, green part only, thinly sliced

Sauce:
1 teaspoon sesame seeds
2½ tablespoons Chinese sesame paste or smooth peanut butter
2 tablespoons cooked peanut oil (heated to smoking, then cooled)
1 tablespoon chile bean sauce
2 teaspoons sesame oil
2 tablespoons chicken stock
1½ tablespoons Chinese black vinegar
1 tablespoon sugar
1 tablespoon soy sauce

Pour boiling water over noodles in a bowl and let stand for 3 to 5 minutes. Drain. Cut noodles roughly with a pair of scissors and toss with 1 teaspoon sesame oil.

To make sauce, lightly toast sesame seeds in a dry, hot pan. Combine sesame paste, cooked peanut oil, chile bean sauce, and sesame oil until it forms a paste. Stir in chicken stock, black vinegar, sugar, and soy sauce and sprinkle sesame seeds on top. Set aside.

Put chicken in a large saucepan with a snug-fitting lid and just cover with cold water. Remove chicken and bring water to a boil. Return chicken to the water, reduce heat until water is barely simmering, and cover tightly. Simmer for 30 minutes, or until fully cooked.

Remove chicken from the pot and plunge into a large bowl of icy-cold water. Lift out and replunge 3 or 4 times, which will give the chicken a marvelously smooth texture. Brush chicken with remaining 1 teaspoon sesame oil. Remove chicken meat from the bones and shred it finely.

Put noodles on a large serving plate. Arrange shredded chicken on top, and pour the sauce over, serving any extra sauce in a small bowl for dipping. Scatter with green onions and serve.

Serves 4

noodle ID 11

Eight Treasure Noodles

To the Chinese, eight is a significant and lucky number because the word for eight sounds very much like the word for prosperous. For this reason, celebratory banquets will often officially consist of eight courses (even if a few extras are thrown in for good measure). In Chinese cooking, there is eight treasure duck, eight treasure chicken, and eight treasure rice, but as far as I know, there have been no eight treasure noodles, until now.

3 tablespoons dried shrimp, soaked in hot water for 30 minutes
6 dried shiitake mushrooms, soaked in hot water for 30 minutes
2 tablespoons peanut oil
2 lup cheong sausages, thinly sliced
½ cup lotus seeds or gingko nuts (available canned)
½ onion, finely diced
½ cup bamboo shoots, cut into matchsticks
2 tablespoons dark soy sauce
2 teaspoons sesame oil
1 teaspoon salt
½ teaspoon five-spice powder
3 ounces char sieu (red roast pork), cut into thin strips
1 cooked chicken thigh, cut into thin strips
1 cup chicken stock
1 teaspoon cornstarch
1 tablespoon shaohsing rice wine or dry sherry
11 ounces dried wheat noodles
2 green onions, green part only, thinly sliced

Drain dried shrimp and mushrooms. Cut off and discard mushroom stems and thinly slice caps. Heat peanut oil in a hot wok and stir-fry shrimp, mushrooms, sausage, lotus seeds, onion, and bamboo shoots for 2 minutes. Add soy sauce, sesame oil, salt, and five-spice powder.

Add pork, chicken, and chicken stock and cook, stirring, for 1 minute. Mix cornstarch into rice wine and stir into the mixture. Cook for 1 minute until sauce thickens slightly.

Meanwhile, cook noodles in plenty of boiling water for 3 to 4 minutes. Drain and combine with the sauce, tossing well. Serve on a large warmed platter or in small Chinese bowls, with green onions scattered over the top.

Serves 4

noodle ID 1

japan

Spring Rain Tempura 93

Chilled Somen 94

Curry Udon 95

Memories of Shikoku Udon 97

Fox Noodles with Chicken and Mushrooms 98

Nabeyaki Udon 99

Zaru Soba 101

Sukiyaki 102

Tempura Soba 103

Somen with Salt-Grilled Snapper 105

Odamaki Mushi 106

Ramen with Char Sieu 107

Moon-Viewing Noodles 108

Japan–Modern

Teriyaki Salmon with Udon and Spinach 109

Soba with Eggplant and Miso 110

Five Mushroom Miso with Ramen 111

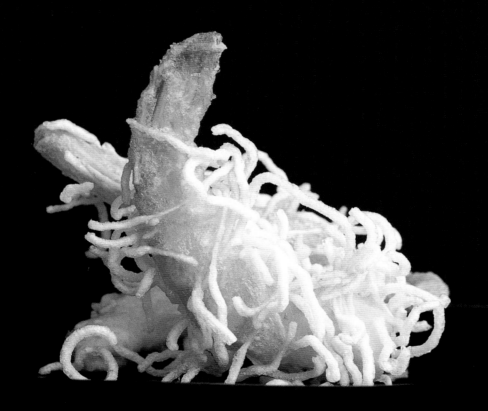

Spring Rain Tempura

Harusame noodles, also known as "spring rain," are usually served in salads and soups, but they also have the ability to puff up quite dramatically when deep-fried. This unusual tempura recipe makes the most of that ability, giving the seafood an almost theatrical appearance.

¾ cup flour
2 egg whites
3 ounces harusame noodles
Vegetable oil, for deep-frying
13 ounces white fish fillets, cut into 6-inch pieces
12 medium shrimp, peeled and deveined
2 green bell peppers, cut into 1-inch strips

Dipping sauce:
1 cup dashi (see Basics, page 191)
⅓ cup mirin
⅓ cup light soy sauce
2 tablespoons grated daikon (white radish)

Put flour in a shallow bowl. In another bowl, beat egg whites until frothy, but not stiff and peaky. Put noodles in a large plastic bag, cut into ½-inch lengths inside the bag (to keep the pieces from flying across the room as you cut), and put into another bowl.

To make dipping sauce, combine dashi, mirin, and soy sauce in a small saucepan and bring to a boil. Remove from heat and pour into 4 individual bowls, adding a little of the grated daikon to each.

Pour enough oil for deep-frying into a hot wok or saucepan and heat until a cube of bread dances on the surface, turning golden within 5 seconds. Roll fish, shrimp, and bell pepper strips first in flour, then in egg white, then in harusame noodles. Drop coated pieces into the oil, 3 at a time. The noodles will puff out dramatically. Fry until cooked through and noodles are pale gold. Remove and drain well. Continue the process until all seafood and vegetable pieces are fried. (Whisk the egg white briskly before each dipping to keep it frothy.)

Arrange seafood and vegetables on small serving plates, and serve with dipping sauce.

Serves 4

noodle ID 16

Chilled Somen

An exceptionally refreshing summer dish, this is the Zen of cold noodles in a single bowl—pared back, subtle, yet with intriguing and satisfying layers of flavor. Resist the temptation to overcook the noodles, as they need to retain an almost al dente bite to keep the diner's interest.

7 ounces somen
6 dried shiitake mushrooms, soaked in hot water for an hour
1½ cups dashi (see Basics, page 191)
½ cup mirin
5 tablespoons soy sauce
1 small cucumber, cut into matchsticks
1 handful of watercress, blanched
2 green onions, finely chopped
1 teaspoon prepared wasabi

Put noodles in a pot of boiling water. When water returns to a boil, add ½ cup of cold water. When it starts to boil again, add another ½ cup of cold water. After about 2 minutes of cooking, the noodles should be ready. Rinse in plenty of cold water and drain. Refrigerate for about 2 hours.

Drain mushrooms and cut off stems.

To make the dipping sauce, combine dashi, mirin, soy sauce, and mushrooms in a saucepan and simmer for 5 minutes. Remove mushrooms and cut in half.

Strain liquid and cool quickly by pouring it into a bowl sitting in another bowl filled with iced water. Refrigerate until well chilled.

Divide noodles among 4 Japanese plates or bowls and top with cucumber strips, a little mound of watercress, 2 mushroom halves, and a sprinkling of green onions. Serve with individual bowls of dipping sauce and a little wasabi for adding to individual taste.

Serves 4

noodle ID 14

Curry Udon

The Japanese have adopted the idea of curry in much the same way they adopted the art of deep-frying from the Portuguese, and the art of crumbing from Eastern Europe. Curry powder first came to Japan in the late 19th century and, while in no way resembling Indian cookery, Japanese curries have a peculiar charm all their own.

10 ounces dried udon
2 tablespoons peanut oil
2 onions, sliced
11 ounces boneless chicken thigh, cut into bite-size cubes
1 cup green beans, blanched
3 teaspoons curry powder
4 cups chicken stock
1 teaspoon sugar
3 tablespoons tapioca flour or potato starch
2 green onions, finely sliced

Put noodles in a pot of boiling water. When water returns to a boil, add 1 cup cold water. When water again returns to a boil, add another cup cold water. Repeat the process another 2 to 4 times, depending on thickness of udon, until the noodles are cooked but still have a little resilience. Drain, rinse in cold water, and set aside.

Heat oil in a saucepan and fry onions gently for a couple of minutes. Add chicken and cook for 1 minute, then add beans and cook for another minute. Sprinkle on curry powder and mix in with a wooden spoon. Pour in chicken stock and sugar, bring to a boil, and simmer for 3 minutes. Mix tapioca flour with a little water. Drizzle mixture into the pot, stirring thoroughly. Cook until the mixture boils and starts to thicken.

Pour boiling water over noodles in a colander or strainer in the sink. Drain well and distribute warmed noodles among 4 individual bowls. Pour sauce over noodles and scatter with green onions.

Serves 4

Memories of Shikoku Udon

To travel around Shikoku, Japan's southernmost island, is to discover the Japan that existed long before neon signs, mini-computers, and conveyor-belt sushi. It was here that I had my first taste of kamaboko, *a fish paste so superior that it even tasted delicious at the crack of dawn. It was also my first serious encounter with udon noodles, the proudest product of Kamogowa, on the northern coast. This is my homage to these two wonderful creations.*

8 dried shiitake mushrooms, soaked in hot water for an hour
9 ounces dried udon noodles
1 tablespoon dried wakame (seaweed)
6 ounces Japanese fish cake (kamaboko)
2 green onions, green part only
9 ounces fresh tofu
6 cups dashi (see Basics, page 191)
4 tablespoons light soy sauce
3 tablespoons mirin
2 teaspoons sugar
4 hard-boiled eggs, sliced but kept in egg shape

Drain mushrooms, remove stems, slice each cap into 3 or 4 strips, and set aside.

Bring a large pot of water to a boil and add noodles. When water returns to a boil, add 1 cup of cold water. When water again returns to a boil, add another cup of cold water. Repeat the process once or twice more until noodles are soft, but not sloppy. Rinse in plenty of cold running water, drain, and set aside.

Soak wakame in lukewarm water and leave to swell for about 10 minutes. Drain and set aside. Cut fish cake into thin slices. Cut green onions into 2½-inch lengths. Drain tofu, cut into 12 even cubes, and set aside.

Bring dashi to a boil with soy sauce, mirin, and sugar. Add mushrooms and tofu and simmer for 5 minutes. Add fish cake slices and simmer for 3 to 4 minutes. Add wakame and green onions and heat through.

Rinse noodles with boiling water to heat them, drain thoroughly, and distribute among 4 large soup bowls. Ladle soup over noodles, including the fish cake, wakame, tofu, and mushrooms. Arrange a sliced egg on top of each bowl, fanning out the slices, and serve immediately, with chopsticks and spoons.

Serves 4

noodle ID 13

Fox Noodles with Chicken and Mushrooms

The name of this dish—kitsune udon—translates as fox noodles, apparently because of the wily beast's fondness for fried tofu. I don't think this assertion has ever been scientifically proven, but it's such a nice story that I'm prepared to go along with it. This is done in the Osaka style, which just means it has chicken in it. Aburage, fried dried sheets of tofu, are available frozen from Japanese supermarkets.

4 sheets aburage (fried dried tofu sheets)
8 dried shiitake mushrooms, soaked in hot water for an hour
10 ounces boneless chicken, cut into 1-inch cubes
8 ounces dried udon noodles
2 green onions, thinly sliced

Simmering Broth:
2 cups dashi (see Basics, page 191)
2 tablespoons soy sauce
1 tablespoon sugar

Noodle Broth:
6 cups dashi (see Basics, page 191)
2 tablespoons soy sauce
1 tablespoon mirin
1 teaspoon sugar
½ teaspoon salt

Cut each aburage sheet in half on the diagonal to create 8 triangles. Pour boiling water over aburage to remove the oil, then drain and combine with simmering broth ingredients in a saucepan. Bring to a boil, lower heat, and simmer, covered, for 10 minutes, then remove aburage from broth.

Drain mushrooms and remove stems.

In a separate saucepan, combine noodle broth ingredients, bring to a boil, and simmer for 2 minutes. Add chicken and mushrooms and simmer for 3 minutes, or until chicken is just cooked through. Skim if necessary.

Bring a large pot of water to a boil and add noodles. When water returns to a boil, add 1 cup of cold water. When water returns to a boil again, add another cup of cold water, then continue to boil until noodles are one step past al dente (firm, but cooked through).

Drain noodles and rinse with boiling water. Divide among 4 deep soup bowls and pour hot soup on top. Add 2 triangles of aburage to each bowl, along with a little pile of green onions.

Serves 4

noodle ID 13

Nabeyaki Udon

This dish is often called noodles in a pot because of the heavy, cast-iron, heat-retaining pot in which the dish is cooked. You'll find these pots at most good Japanese food stores, although a heatproof casserole will do the job as well.

4 dried shiitake mushrooms, soaked in hot water for an hour
7 ounces dried udon noodles
2 chicken thighs
4 tablespoons soy sauce
3 tablespoons mirin
1 tablespoon dried wakame (seaweed)
4 cups dashi (see Basics, page 191)
1 tablespoon sugar
Pinch of salt
3 ounces Japanese fish cake (kamaboko), thinly sliced
vegetable oil, for deep-frying
4 large shrimp, peeled (leaving tails on) and deveined
1 cup flour
1 quantity tempura batter (see Basics, page 191)
1 egg
1 green onion, cut into 2 ½-inch lengths

Drain mushrooms, cut off stems, and slice caps in half.

Place noodles in plenty of water at a rolling boil. Add 1 cup of cold water. When water returns to a boil, add another cup of cold water. Repeat the process once or twice more until noodles are soft, but not sloppy. Rinse in plenty of cold running water, drain, and set aside.

Cut chicken meat from bone and cut into bite-size pieces. Marinate with 1 tablespoon soy sauce and 1 tablespoon mirin for 30 minutes. Soak wakame in lukewarm water for 10 minutes, drain, and set aside.

In a round, heatproof casserole, combine dashi, remaining soy sauce, remaining mirin, sugar, and salt and bring to a boil. Add chicken, mushrooms, and fish cake slices and simmer for 15 minutes.

Heat oil in a hot wok until just smoking. Dredge shrimp in flour, then in the tempura batter and drop straight into the hot oil. Deep-fry for about 2 minutes, or until batter turns lightly golden and crisp.

Rinse noodles in boiling water, add to the soup, and bring to a boil. Break egg into the soup, add green onion and wakame, and cover for about a minute, cooking over high heat until egg white is cooked but yolk is still runny. Add the tempura shrimp and bring pot to the table for sharing. Traditionally, the egg is then broken with chopsticks and stirred through the soup, creating a creamy broth.

Serves 2 as a meal, or 4 as
part of a meal

Zaru Soba

A zaru is a bamboo basket or slatted bamboo box. Originally, soba noodles were made entirely from buckwheat and were susceptible to breaking, so they were normally steamed and then served in the zaru. These days, with the addition of wheat flour, soba noodles are strong enough to withstand boiling. Nevertheless, they are still served in the traditional zaru.

8 ounces dried soba
2 cups dashi (see Basics, page 191)
¼ cup soy sauce
¼ cup mirin
½ teaspoon sugar
1 sheet nori (dried seaweed)
1 teaspoon wasabi powder, mixed to a paste with a little water
3 green onions, thinly sliced

Bring water to a boil, add soba, and when water returns to a boil, add 1 cup cold water. When water again returns to a boil, add another cup cold water. Repeat the process another 2 to 4 times, depending on the thickness of the soba, until the noodles are cooked but still resilient. Rinse thoroughly in cold water and reserve.

Bring dashi, soy sauce, mirin, and sugar to a boil, stirring until sugar has dissolved. Cool and chill this dipping sauce in refrigerator.

When ready to serve, divide noodles among 4 shallow bowls or slatted bamboo boxes. Lightly toast nori over a gas flame or under broiler until crisp, cut with scissors into long, thin strips, and scatter over noodles.

Divide chilled dipping sauce among 4 small serving bowls. Each diner picks up some noodles with chopsticks and dips them into the dipping sauce, adding wasabi and green onions to their personal taste.

Serves 4

Sukiyaki

Although this one-pot beef and vegetable dish is now regarded as Japan's national dish, beef wasn't eaten in Japan until the 1860s, when it was introduced by homesick Westerners. As with most of the ideas the Japanese "borrowed" from the West, they simply forgot to give it back. Steamed rice and pickles are generally served toward the end of the meal.

5 ounces fresh silken tofu
8 dried shiitake mushrooms
7 ounces shirataki noodles
7 ounces Chinese cabbage
4 green onions
1 bunch enoki mushrooms
1 onion, thinly sliced
1 pound eye fillet or sirloin beef, sliced wafer-thin
4 eggs
3 ounces beef suet

Sauce:
¾ cup dashi (see Basics, page 191)
¾ cup soy sauce
¾ cup mirin
3 tablespoons sugar

Cut tofu into 1-inch cubes. Soak shiitake mushrooms in hot water for 1 hour, drain, and remove and discard stems. Drain shirataki noodles and cook in a pot of boiling water for 1 to 2 minutes. Drain again.

Slice cabbage into 1½-inch sections and quarter each section. Cut green onions into 2-inch pieces. Arrange cabbage, tofu, green onions, noodles, mushrooms, and onion with sliced beef on a large platter.

In a small saucepan, combine sauce ingredients and heat, stirring, until sugar has dissolved. Transfer to a pitcher. Place a whole egg in each of 4 Japanese bowls. Each diner cracks the egg into his or her bowl and beats it lightly with chopsticks.

Put a sukiyaki pan, or a good, heavy-bottomed iron pan, on a portable table stove (or use an electric frying pan). Rub the bottom of the pot with suet. Add onion and let cook for a few minutes. Add beef slices and a little of all the other ingredients and pour some of the sauce over. Be careful not to let the beef overcook (1 minute is plenty). Each diner then selects a piece of meat or vegetable from the pan, dips it quickly in the egg and eats it. Keep replenishing pan as you go.

Serves 4

Tempura Soba

The Japanese love adding crisp tempura to noodle soups. Personally, I like to serve the tempura separately at the table and let each person add it while still crisp and crunchy to the soup, but that's a very un-Japanese thing to do.

14 ounces dried soba
Vegetable oil, for deep-frying
8 shrimp, peeled (leaving tails on) and deveined
8 scallops
½ bell pepper, cut lengthwise into 4 strips
1 quantity tempura batter (see Basics, page 191)
6 cups dashi (see Basics, page 191)
2 tablespoons mirin
1 tablespoon light soy sauce
1 green onion, sliced

Bring water to a boil, add soba, and when water returns to a boil, add 1 cup cold water. When water again returns to a boil, add another cup cold water. Repeat the process another 2 to 4 times, depending on the thickness of the soba, until the noodles are cooked but still resilient. Drain, rinse in cold water, and set aside for use.

Heat oil in a hot wok until a cube of bread dances on the surface, turning golden within 5 seconds. Dip each piece of seafood and bell pepper into batter and deep-fry until a nice even golden color. Be sure to drain tempura well on paper towels.

When ready to serve, pour boiling water over noodles in a colander to heat, and drain well. Bring dashi to a boil in a saucepan, add mirin and soy sauce, and simmer for 2 minutes. Place some noodles in each of 4 deep bowls and add broth just to the top of the noodles. Add tempura pieces and a little green onion.

Serves 4

noodle ID 12

Somen with Salt-Grilled Snapper

The Japanese have a way with salt grilling that tends to give fish and seafood the very breath of the sea. Not only does salt give a distinctive, crisp texture, but it accentuates the integral flavors of the fish. This dish works with practically any fish, particularly oily varieties, as long as they are fresh.

8 ounces somen noodles
3 cups dashi (see Basics, page 191)
1 tablespoon soy sauce
1 tablespoon mirin
2 teaspoons sea salt
½ teaspoon sugar
6 fresh shiitake mushrooms, stemmed (optional)
2 skin-on snapper fillets, about 8 ounces each
Sea salt, for grilling
2 green onions, chopped

Put somen in a pot of boiling water. When water returns to a boil, add ½ cup cold water. When it again returns to a boil, add another ½ cup cold water. After about 2 minutes of cooking, noodles should be ready. Rinse well under cold water, drain, and set aside.

Bring dashi to a boil with soy sauce, mirin, salt, and sugar, add mushrooms, and simmer for 3 to 4 minutes. Remove from heat and set aside.

Cut and trim each fillet into 2 neat almost-squares. Thread a bamboo skewer up one side of each square, so that it looks like a flag. Thread another skewer up the other side. This will keep the fillets flat while they grill. Scatter a little sea salt on a chopping board and place fish, skin side down, on the salt. Sprinkle a little more salt over the flesh side and leave for 5 minutes. Place on a hot charcoal grill and cook, skin side down, until fish is three-quarters done. Turn and cook on the other side for a minute or two.

Remove mushrooms from broth and cut into thin slivers. Pour boiling water through reserved noodles in a strainer to heat.

Divide noodles among 4 shallow bowls, scatter with mushroom slivers, and pour broth into each bowl. Remove fish from skewers and place over each noodle pile. Scatter with green onions and serve.

Serves 4

Odamaki Mushi

This delicate Japanese custard is traditionally made in pretty, lidded pots, as for chawan mushi. Small ramekins tightly covered with plastic wrap won't have the same table theater, but will work just as well.

4 medium shrimp, peeled and deveined
Pinch of sea salt
1 small chicken breast, cut into ½-inch cubes
1 teaspoon sake
1 tablespoon plus 1 teaspoon soy sauce
4 eggs
1 tablespoon mirin
2¼ cups dashi, chilled (see Basics, page 191)
16 cooked udon noodles
2 water chestnuts, thinly sliced
2 dried shiitake mushrooms, soaked in hot water for an hour, drained, stemmed, and
    halved
20 enoki mushrooms
1 green onion, green part only, thinly sliced

In two separate bowls, sprinkle shrimp with sea salt, and marinate diced chicken with sake and 1 teaspoon soy sauce. Set aside.

Beat eggs lightly in a bowl with a fork, being careful not to let the mixture froth and bubble. Add remaining 1 tablespoon soy sauce and mirin to the cold dashi and pour liquid into the eggs in a slow, steady stream, gently folding with a wooden spoon as you go. Again, it should be mixed well, but without creating bubbles.

Place 4 noodles each at the bottom of 4 lidded bowls. Add chicken, shrimp, water chestnuts, and mushrooms and pour in the egg and dashi mixture to about ½ inch from the top. Cover each with a lid and wrap with plastic wrap, or cover ramekins with plastic wrap, and place in a steamer over moderate to high heat for about 20 to 25 minutes. Alternatively, set the pots in a baking tray half-filled with water and cook for up to 30 minutes in an oven heated to 425°.

When custards are set, but still retain a wobble, they are ready to serve. Top each custard with a little green onion, replace lids, and serve with Japanese spoons and chopsticks.

Serves 4

noodle ID 13

Ramen with Char Sieu

It is ironic to note that the most popular noodles in Japan are not Japanese, but the Chinese-style ramen wheat noodles. This dish borrows again from the Chinese in the form of char sieu, gloriously red roast pork, which you'll find hanging in the window of every Chinese barbecued meat shop.

12 ounces fresh ramen noodles
8 ounces char sieu (red roast pork)
2 hard-boiled eggs
24 fresh spinach leaves
6 cups chicken stock
1 tablespoon soy sauce
½ teaspoon sugar
½ teaspoon salt
8 slices Japanese fish cake (kamaboko)
16 pieces menma (pickled bamboo shoot)
2 green onions, finely sliced

Boil noodles in plenty of simmering water for 2 to 3 minutes. Rinse in cold water, drain, and reserve.

Thinly slice pork and eggs. Blanch spinach in boiling water for 20 seconds. Put stock in a saucepan, add soy sauce, sugar, and salt, and bring to a boil. Add fish cake slices, simmer for 2 minutes, and remove.

Pour boiling water over noodles in a strainer to heat. Divide them among 4 large soup bowls and pour stock over. Carefully arrange pork, fish cake, spinach, menma, and sliced egg on top. Scatter with green onions and serve.

Serves 4

Moon-Viewing Noodles

Of course that's not a mysterious moon drifting meaningfully through the clouds. It's a raw egg. If you can see the beauty in that, too, then you're ready to appreciate tsukimi udon, *which is a great favorite in a country where moon-viewing is a popular family pastime. If you're not sure about eating a very lightly set egg, poach the eggs separately to your liking and slip them into the soup at the last moment.*

13 ounces fresh, cooked, or instant udon noodles
4 dried shiitake mushrooms, soaked in hot water for an hour
6 cups dashi (see Basics, page 191)
2 tablespoons light soy sauce
1 tablespoon mirin
4 fresh eggs
8 slices Japanese fish cake (kamaboko)
½ sheet nori (dried seaweed)
2 large green onions, thinly sliced on the diagonal

Pour boiling water over noodles in a large bowl and gently separate them with chopsticks. Drain, rinse under cold water, and drain again.

Drain mushrooms, remove and discard stems, and slice caps in half.

Bring dashi to a boil in a saucepan with soy sauce and mirin and simmer for 3 minutes. Reheat noodles briefly in boiling water, then divide among 4 warmed serving bowls, making a little hollow nest in each pile.

Add enough boiling broth to come halfway up the noodles, then break an egg into each nest. Arrange fish cake and mushrooms to one side and carefully ladle more boiling broth on top just to cover the egg. Immediately cover each bowl with a plate and leave for 2 minutes before removing it.

Toast nori over a gas flame or under broiler for a few seconds until it crisps. Cut into thin strips and scatter over the top of the noodles with green onions.

Serves 4

noodle ID 13

Teriyaki Salmon with Udon and Spinach

The whole idea of teriyaki grilling is devilishly clever. Sugar and sake are added to the basting liquid not just for the distinctive flavor, but to achieve that glamorous glazed look and to encourage those highly desirable scorched brown bits.

8 cups dashi (see Basics, page 191)
2 tablespoons soy sauce
2 tablespoons mirin
1 knob fresh ginger
13 ounces dried udon
4 small salmon fillets, skinned
1 bunch spinach, washed
4 green onions, sliced on the diagonal

Teriyaki Sauce:
2 tablespoons dark soy sauce
1 tablespoon sake
1 tablespoon mirin
1 tablespoon peanut oil
1 teaspoon sugar

For teriyaki sauce, combine dark soy, sake, mirin, oil, and sugar in a small pot and heat, stirring, until sugar has dissolved. Set aside.

Heat dashi in a second pot and add soy and mirin. Peel ginger, cut into cubes, and crush in a garlic press to get 1 tablespoon ginger juice. Add juice to broth and adjust flavorings to taste.

Cook noodles in plenty of boiling water until al dente, about 8 minutes. Drain and rinse in cold water, cover with plastic wrap, and set aside.

Brush salmon with teriyaki sauce and grill quickly on a hot, well-oiled grill, leaving inside lightly pink. Bring dashi broth to just below a boil. Add noodles to broth for 30 seconds to heat through, then divide noodles among 4 warmed bowls. Dip spinach leaves briefly in broth to wilt them, and distribute among the bowls. Ladle hot broth into each bowl and top noodles with grilled salmon. Scatter green onions on top and serve with chopsticks and spoons.

Serves 4

Soba with Eggplant and Miso

We tend to think of eggplant as a Mediterranean vegetable, yet nobody explores its potential more thoroughly or more joyously than the Japanese. The combination of eggplant and red miso is a triumph of compatibility. I'm sure I'm not the first person to think of adding the sweet nuttiness of soba noodles to this traditional pairing, served at room temperature.

10 ounces dried soba noodles
1 teaspoon sesame oil
2 medium eggplants
2 tablespoons peanut oil
²⁄₃ cup dashi (see Basics, page 191)
3 tablespoons red miso
3 tablespoons sugar
2 teaspoons sesame seeds
1 green onion, finely chopped

Add soba to plenty of boiling water. When water returns to a boil, add 1 cup cold water. When water again returns to a boil, add another cup cold water. Repeat 2 to 4 times, until the noodles are cooked, but still resilient. Rinse under cold water. Drain well, mix with sesame oil, and set aside.

Wash and trim eggplants and cut into bite-size chunks. Heat peanut oil in a frying pan and cook eggplant, stirring, until the flesh is almost translucent. Add dashi, cover, and simmer for 5 minutes. Add a little of the liquid to the miso in a small bowl and whisk well. Stir in sugar and whisk until it dissolves. Drizzle this mixture slowly over eggplant, stirring well, and simmer for another minute or two until eggplant is tender.

Put noodles in a strainer or colander and pour boiling water over to heat them. Drain well. Arrange noodles on each plate and top with a ladleful of eggplant and sauce. Scatter sesame seeds and green onion over and serve.

Serves 4

Five Mushroom Miso with Ramen

Ten years ago, this dish would have been impossible to make outside Japan, as the only mushrooms we could lay our hands on were button mushrooms or dried shiitakes. Actually, it would still have worked, but it's so much better this way.

14 ounces fresh ramen noodles
1 tablespoon dried wakame (seaweed)
3 ounces silken tofu
10 dried shiitake mushrooms, soaked in hot water for an hour
6 cups dashi (see Basics, page 191)
6 tablespoons red miso
2 tablespoons mirin
8 fresh shiitake mushrooms
1 bunch enoki mushrooms, separated
½ cup shimeji mushrooms, separated
4 oyster mushrooms, cut into thin strips
12 large spinach leaves, stems removed
1 green onion, green part only, cut into 1½-inch lengths.

Cook noodles in boiling water for a minute, rinse under cold water, drain, and reserve. Soak wakame in lukewarm water and leave to swell for 10 minutes. Drain tofu and cut into ½-inch cubes.

Drain mushrooms, remove and discard stems, and slice caps in half.

Bring dashi to a boil in a saucepan. Whisk 2 tablespoons hot dashi into the miso in a bowl, and whisk until well blended. Little by little, pour miso back into the dashi, stirring. Add mirin and simmer over low heat for 2 to 3 minutes.

Add tofu and all the mushrooms and cook for 2 or 3 minutes. Add spinach and cook for up to 1 minute, until it wilts. Add wakame and remove from heat.

Pour boiling water over noodles in a colander or strainer to heat through. Drain and distribute noodles among 4 deep serving bowls. Use tongs to distribute wilted spinach leaves among the bowls, then ladle soup and mushrooms over the top. Top each bowl with green onion.

Serves 4

malaysia

Char Kueh Teow	115
Curry Mee	116
Hokkien Mee	117
Indian Mee Goreng	118
Mee Rebus	119
Mee Siam	120
Penang Laksa	121
Laksa Lemak	123
Singapore Beehoon	124

Malaysia-Modern

Chile Shrimp Noodles	125

Char Kueh Teow

There are two secrets to this dish. One is not to crowd your wok—too many noodles and you'll steam more than stir-fry. The second is heat. Keep the heat high and the noodles moving, and the dish takes on a dark, almost scorched flavor known as "the breath of the wok."

1 lup cheong sausage
1 pound fresh rice sheet noodles
1 teaspoon peanut oil
3 tablespoons vegetable oil
2 cloves of garlic, crushed with the side of a knife blade
3 dried red chiles, soaked, drained, and chopped
12 shrimp, peeled and deveined
7 ounces squid tubes, cleaned and thinly sliced
3 ounces char sieu (red roast pork), sliced into thin strips
1 cup bean sprouts, blanched for 30 seconds
2 tablespoons dark soy sauce
2 tablespoons light soy sauce
1 tablespoon oyster sauce
2 eggs, beaten
4 green onions, finely chopped

Place lup cheong sausage in a steamer and cook for 3 to 4 minutes. Allow to cool, then slice thinly on the diagonal and set aside.

Cut noodles into strips ¾ inch wide and place in a bowl. Pour boiling water over and gently pull them apart with a pair of chopsticks. Drain immediately and rinse under cold water to prevent overcooking. Drain well and mix with 1 teaspoon peanut oil to prevent sticking.

Heat vegetable oil in a hot wok and stir-fry garlic and chiles for 30 seconds. Add shrimp, squid, pork, and sausage and stir-fry for another 2 minutes. Add bean sprouts and cook for a further minute. Remove contents from wok and set aside.

Put a little more oil in the wok, if necessary. Add noodles, dark and light soy sauce, and oyster sauce and toss over high heat for a minute or two, before returning the other ingredients to the wok.

Push noodles to one side of the wok, pour eggs in the space provided, cover with the noodles, and toss to distribute the eggs. Scatter with green onions and serve hot.

Serves 4

noodle ID 7

Curry Mee

Malaysians love to breakfast on this thick, hearty hawker-style curry dish. There is a seafood version using shrimp, clams, and fish balls, but clams may be a little hard to take at breakfast if you're used to toast and jam.

1 small chicken (about 2 pounds)
1 cup green beans, cut into 2-inch lengths
1 tablespoon peanut oil
6 shallots, coarsely chopped
4 candlenuts or macadamia nuts
1 teaspoon grated fresh turmeric, or ½ teaspoon ground turmeric
1 slice ginger, chopped
1 slice galangal, chopped
2 stalks lemongrass, white part only, sliced
2 dried chiles, soaked overnight, drained and chopped
1 teaspoon shrimp paste (belacan)
3 cloves garlic, chopped
2 cups thick coconut milk
4 squares fried bean curd puffs, halved diagonally
1 teaspoon sugar
½ teaspoon salt
4 cups chicken stock
1 pound Hokkien noodles
2 cups bean sprouts
2 hard-boiled eggs, quartered
2 limes, cut into wedges
2 fresh red chiles, sliced
3 tablespoons crisp-fried shallots (available from Asian grocery stores)

Remove meat from chicken and chop into bite-size pieces. Blanch green beans in simmering water for 1 minute, refresh in cold water, and drain. Heat oil in a nonstick frying pan and fry chicken until it colors a little. Remove from heat.

Pound or blend shallots, nuts, turmeric, ginger, galangal, lemongrass, dried chiles, shrimp paste, and garlic to a smooth paste. Scoop 3 tablespoons of thick coconut cream off the top of the milk and heat in a hot wok. Add paste and fry until it smells warm and fragrant. Add chicken pieces, green beans, bean curd puffs, sugar, and salt, followed by the remaining coconut milk and stock, and simmer over low heat until chicken is cooked, about 10 minutes.

Pour boiling water over noodles in a bowl and let stand for 30 seconds. Drain and distribute noodles among 4 deep soup bowls. Put some bean sprouts on top and ladle chicken and curry over. Serve topped with the egg quarters, lime wedges, fresh red chiles, and crisp-fried shallots.

Serves 4

Hokkien Mee

One of the great standards of Malaysian hawker-stall cooking, with every merchant claiming to have the one, the true, the authentic recipe. There is a popular, darker version of the dish, to which oyster sauce and dark soy are added, but I prefer this lighter variation, which gives the subtle flavors of the squid and shrimp a chance to star.

7 ounces fresh Hokkien egg noodles
3 ounces rice vermicelli
7 ounces squid tubes, cleaned
3 tablespoons peanut oil
2 eggs, beaten
2 cloves garlic, crushed with the side of a knife blade
12 shrimp, peeled and deveined
3 ounces char sieu (red roast pork), diced
2 cups bean sprouts, washed
1 cup hot chicken stock, or stock made from shrimp shells
2 tablespoons light soy sauce

Pour boiling water over Hokkien noodles in a bowl, let stand for a minute, then drain and rinse. Pour boiling water over rice vermicelli in a bowl and let stand for 6 to 7 minutes. Rinse under cold water, drain, and set aside.

Cut squid into 1-inch squares and score lightly with the tip of a knife.

Heat 1 tablespoon oil in a hot wok and swirl around to coat the surface. Pour in beaten eggs and quickly swirl around the pan to form a thin omelet. When cooked on one side, gently separate the edge of the omelet from the wok with a knife. Place a plate over the wok and invert the whole thing so that the omelet drops onto the plate. Slide the omelet back in and quickly cook the other side. Flip omelet onto cutting board, roll up into a tight roll, and slice across into thin strips.

Heat remaining oil in the hot wok and stir-fry garlic for 1 minute. Add squid and shrimp and stir-fry for 2 minutes. Add pork, omelet strips, and bean sprouts and stir-fry for a minute. Add noodles, stock, and soy sauce and toss through until hot.

Serves 4

noodle ID 3, 8

Indian Mee Goreng

The great thing about multicultural Malaysia is that every ethnic group gets a chance to influence the local cuisine. This dish came from the Indian street vendors who gave their own unique twist to the Chinese noodle that was adopted by the local Malays as their own. Don't even think about trying to find this dish in India.

13 ounces fresh Hokkien noodles
2 tablespoons vegetable oil
1 onion, sliced
2 boiled potatoes, cut into small cubes
2 tomatoes, cut into small cubes
1 cup small shrimp, cooked and peeled
5 ounces dried bean curd (taukwa), cut into cubes
½ cup bean sprouts
2 tablespoons ketchup
1 tablespoon chile sauce
Salt to taste
Sugar to taste
1 egg, beaten
2 green onions, sliced
½ cup shredded lettuce
1 lime, quartered
2 tablespoons crisp-fried shallots (available from Asian grocery stores)

Pour boiling water over noodles, let stand 1 minute, drain, rinse, and set aside.

Heat oil in a hot wok and fry onion until soft. Add noodles and cook for 2 minutes. Add potatoes, tomatoes, shrimp, bean curd cake, bean sprouts, ketchup, and chile sauce and cook over high heat, stirring, until well mixed. Add salt and sugar to taste.

Tilt wok, push noodles to one side, pour in egg, cover with noodles, and leave to cook for 30 seconds. Toss well, add green onions, and toss again. Serve topped with shredded lettuce, lime wedges, and crisp-fried shallots.

Serves 4

Mee Rebus

Sweet potato might not be the first ingredient that pops into your mind when you think about making a sauce for noodles, but when Malay hawker-stall cooks use it to thicken this full-on gravy, the results are nothing short of miraculous.

6 shallots, chopped
5 candlenuts or macadamia nuts, crushed
2 slices fresh ginger, shredded
2 cloves garlic, chopped
3 dried red chiles, chopped
2 slices galangal, chopped
2 tablespoons dried shrimp, ground to a powder
1 tablespoon Malaysian curry powder
2 tablespoons peanut oil
10 ounces good beef (such as tenderloin), thinly sliced
2 tablespoons yellow bean sauce (taucheo)
2 teaspoons sugar
2½ cups beef stock
1 cup mashed boiled sweet potato
13 ounces fresh Hokkien noodles
7 ounces bean sprouts, scalded in boiling water
2 tablespoons crisp-fried shallots (available from Asian grocery stores)
2 red chiles, finely sliced
5 ounces dried bean curd (taukwa), deep fried and sliced
1 cucumber, cut into thin slices
2 green onions, green part only, thinly sliced
2 hard-boiled eggs, quartered

Pound or blend shallots, candlenuts, ginger, garlic, chopped dried chiles, galangal, shrimp powder, and curry powder to a thick paste. Heat peanut oil in a hot wok and fry paste until it is warmly fragrant. Add beef and cook for 2 minutes. Add yellow bean sauce and sugar, stir through, then add stock and sweet potato. Mix well.

Cover noodles with boiling water in a bowl. Let stand for 30 seconds, then drain. Put noodles and bean sprouts in 4 large individual bowls and pour the sauce over. Top with crisp-fried shallots, sliced red chiles, bean curd slices, cucumber, green onions, and hard-boiled egg quarters.

Serves 4

noodle ID 3

Mee Siam

Created by Nonya Malaysian cooks inspired by the noodle dishes of Thailand. With its nice, fresh, sweet-salty flavors, it winds up being neither really Thai nor Malaysian, but something that forms a bridge of good taste between the two.

10 ounces rice vermicelli
10 dried red chiles, soaked, drained, and chopped
2 tablespoons dried shrimp, ground to a powder
1 tablespoon shrimp paste (belacan)
1 tablespoon finely chopped shallots
3 tablespoons peanut oil
8 ounces shrimp, peeled and deveined
1 cup water
1 tablespoon sugar
1 teaspoon salt
1 teaspoon oyster sauce
2 cups bean sprouts

Sauce:
¼ cup yellow bean sauce (taucheo), lightly mashed
2 tablespoons sugar
1 onion, thinly sliced
2 tablespoons tamarind water (see Glossary, page 197)
3 cups coconut milk

To Serve:
3 hard-boiled eggs, quartered
2 limes, quartered
1 tablespoon crisp-fried shallots (available from Asian grocery stores)
2 green onions, cut into 1-inch lengths

Pour boiling water over noodles and let stand for 4 to 5 minutes. Rinse in cold water, drain, and set aside.

Pound or blend chiles, shrimp powder, shrimp paste, and shallot to a fine paste. Heat oil in a hot wok and fry shrimp for 1 minute, until just cooked. Remove shrimp, then add paste and fry until it is fragrant. Remove half the paste and reserve.

Add water, sugar, salt, and oyster sauce to the wok and bring to a boil, stirring. Add bean sprouts and cook for 1 minute. Add noodles and stir-fry for 3 to 4 minutes until liquid is absorbed.

For the sauce, combine ingredients in a saucepan, stir well, and bring to a boil. Add reserved paste and simmer for 5 minutes.

Arrange noodles on a large platter and drizzle with hot sauce. Surround with quartered eggs, shrimp, and lime wedges and sprinkle with crisp-fried shallots and green onions.

Serves 4

noodle ID 8

Penang Laksa

When most people think of laksa, they think of curry laksa or laksa lemak. But the people of Penang have devised their own laksa using fish. Rather than thick, creamy, and coconutty, this laksa is sour and brothy—a totally different kettle of fish.

4 cups cold water
½ teaspoon salt
1 whole (about 1 pound) blue mackerel or other firm-fleshed fish, cleaned
2 cups tamarind water (see Glossary, page 197)
2 stalks lemongrass, white part only, thinly sliced
6 dried chiles, soaked, drained, and chopped
1 tablespoon shrimp paste (belacan)
2 teaspoons ground turmeric
¾-inch piece galangal or ginger, finely chopped
1 tablespoon palm sugar or granulated sugar
10 ounces round rice noodles or Hokkien noodles
1 cucumber, peeled, seeded, and cut into thin matchsticks

Bring water and salt to a boil, add fish, and simmer for 5 minutes, until just cooked. Remove fish, cool, then flake off flesh with your hands and set aside. Return heads and bones to the water. Add tamarind water and simmer for another 10 minutes, then strain through a fine sieve and set stock aside.

Pound or blend lemongrass, chiles, shrimp paste, turmeric, and galangal to a paste. Add to fish stock with sugar and simmer for 10 minutes. Add fish and heat through.

Pour boiling water over noodles in a bowl. Drain and divide noodles among 4 warm serving bowls. Add soup and top with cucumber.

Serves 4

noodle ID 9

Laksa Lemak

This is my number one, very favorite noodle dish in all the world. It has every taste sensation you can think of—tart, salty, sour, sweet, rich, tangy, creamy—and a few others they haven't invented words for yet. While you can buy some perfectly good prepared laksa pastes these days, you never get the same feeling of having really earned your laksa as when you pound the paste yourself.

10 ounces fresh round rice noodles (*or* 7 ounces Hokkien noodles and 3 ounces rice vermicelli)
2 tablespoons vegetable oil
1 quantity laksa paste (see Basics, page 190)
6 cups chicken stock
2 teaspoons palm or brown sugar
1 teaspoon salt
2 cups coconut milk
Meat from half a cooked chicken, sliced
8 fish balls
8 shrimp, peeled and deveined
4 squares fried bean curd puffs, halved diagonally
2 tablespoons slivered bamboo shoots
1 cucumber, peeled, seeded, and cut into matchsticks
1 cup bean sprouts, blanched
Fresh mint and cilantro sprigs, for garnish

Pour boiling water over round rice noodles in a bowl. Drain and rinse. (Alternatively, pour boiling water over Hokkien noodles. Drain and rinse. Cook rice vermicelli in plenty of water at a rolling boil for about 2 minutes. Drain.)

Heat oil in a hot wok and fry laksa paste for about 5 minutes, until fragrant. Add stock, sugar, and salt and bring to a boil. Reduce heat and add coconut milk, stirring constantly as it heats.

Add chicken, fish balls, shrimp, bean curd puffs, and bamboo shoots to the soup, and heat through for a few minutes, until shrimp is cooked, without boiling.

Distribute noodles among 4 deep bowls. Using tongs, distribute fish balls, shrimp, and chicken among the bowls and top with hot soup. Scatter cucumber and bean sprouts on top along with sprigs of mint and cilantro.

Serves 4

noodle ID 9

Singapore Beehoon

Singapore noodles, or Sing chow, *is widely known outside the Lion City, but unheard of in its hometown. More usually it is simply called fried beehoon, after the noodle itself. The popular addition of curry powder is not to my taste, but feel free to add a teaspoon of good, fresh Malaysian curry powder if it is to yours.*

8 ounces rice vermicelli
1 tablespoon vegetable oil
½ onion, or 4 shallots, sliced
1 egg, lightly beaten
1 tablespoon chicken stock or water
3 ounces cooked shredded chicken
3 ounces char sieu (red roast pork), sliced
1 tablespoon dark soy sauce
1 tablespoon light soy sauce
5 ounces shrimp, peeled and deveined
½ cup bean sprouts
2 green onions, finely chopped
½ cup shredded lettuce
1 tablespoon crisp-fried shallots (available from Asian grocery stores)
1 lemon, quartered

Pour boiling water over noodles in a bowl and let stand for 6 to 7 minutes. Rinse in cold water and drain.

Heat oil in a hot wok and fry onion until it starts to soften. Add egg and stir until softly cooked. Add drained noodles and stir constantly to coat with egg. Moisten with stock and cook for 1 minute, then add chicken, pork, and soy sauces and cook for 2 minutes. Add shrimp and cook for 1 minute. Add bean sprouts and green onions and cook for another minute or two. Serve on a large warmed platter, topped with shredded lettuce, crisp-fried shallots, and lemon wedges for squeezing over.

Serves 4

noodle ID 8

Chile Shrimp Noodles

Traditionally, Singapore's famous, finger-licking chile crab and chile shrimp dishes are mopped up with slices of fresh, commercial white bread. In this dish, however, the luscious sweet/spicy sauce comes with its own built-in mopping-up agent in the form of Hokkien noodles. While not strictly authentic, it is strictly delicious.

2 tablespoons peanut oil
1 pound shrimp, peeled and deveined
2½ cups chicken stock
¼ cup ketchup
2 tablespoons sweet chile sauce
1 clove garlic, crushed with the side of a knife blade
1 teaspoon sugar
½ teaspoon salt
1 teaspoon cornstarch, mixed with 1 tablespoon cold water
4 green onions, chopped
1 egg white, beaten
13 ounces fresh Hokkien noodles

Heat peanut oil in a hot wok and fry shrimp for 1 to 2 minutes, until they turn pink. Add chicken stock and simmer for a minute. Add ketchup, chile sauce, garlic, sugar, and salt, and stir well to mix. Add cornstarch paste, bring to a boil, and stir for 1 minute. Add half the green onions and toss well. Slowly drizzle egg white into the sauce (a good trick is to pour it through the tines of a fork), stirring constantly, until the sauce thickens.

Pour boiling water over noodles in a bowl, let stand for 2 minutes, and drain. Arrange on a warmed serving platter and pour shrimp and sauce on top. Scatter with remaining green onions.

Serves 4

noodle ID 3

Noodle Love

Endo Furahashi pushes through the indigo curtain and steps into the little workroom that fronts the bleakness of Takamatsu Street. Tall and thin, in a white chef's outfit, he looks not unlike an udon noodle himself.

He bows a little automatic bow towards the plate glass window, then immediately sets to work mixing the fine white wheat flour with pure, clean Kagawa prefecture water. Within minutes, a small crowd gathers: a businessman in a shiny blue suit, two white-socked schoolgirls, a mother with a baby cradled loosely in her arms, and Yoshiko, her eyes fixed on the willowy young man in the spotless white jacket. Her stare is intense and unblinking, as if she fears that even a momentary pause would cause the chef to disappear from sight.

Whether or not Furahashi-san is aware that the 20-year-old hotel clerk has been standing at the window every day for the past 3 weeks is hard to say, for he rarely acknowledges his audience. Once flour and water are in the young chef's hands, his eyes focus only on his precious udon, and the rest of the world simply has to wait its turn.

So he doesn't notice Yoshiko's little intake of breath as he thrusts his hands into the dough and begins to knead, pushing with the palms, and gathering with the fingers in a kind of sublime culinary sign language.

Yoshiko loves to watch his hands. To her, they are like two strong salmon swimming upstream against a strong white tide. She loves their strength, their sense of purpose, their power.

They are the hands of a strangler, an assassin, a conqueror.

She also loves the way they caress the smooth satin surface of the finished dough in much the same way that the woman beside her touches the forehead of her baby.

They are the hands of an artist, a holy man, a lover.

Alone each night in her bed, she has difficulty remembering his face, or the color of his eyes, or the shine of his hair. But she knows his hands better than the contours of her own body, and even as sleep closes in around her, she wills herself to stay awake just a little longer to further dwell on the long, strong fingers; the one vein that snakes down the back of the right hand; the clean, broad nails; and the little stitch scar below the left thumb.

To a native of the island of Shikoku, udon chefs are hardly a novelty. Yet, on that morning 3 weeks ago, as she rushed from the bus stop to the Takamatsu City Hotel where she worked, it was as if the hands were beckoning her to the window. She watched, mesmerized by their act of creation. When she finally arrived at the hotel, she looked so different, her cheeks flushed and her eyes bright, that the doorman's head turned to watch her go by.

Since then, she has been drawn back every day, timing her arrival or her errands to his udon-making schedule.

Now, the chef picks up the rested dough and, with a few flicks of his wooden rolling pin, transforms it into a large white tablecloth. His hands then gently fold the tablecloth over itself in a large S shape and place it on the cutting board as if it were precious silk.

He picks up the large steel cutting blade. The index finger of his right hand rubs curiously along the edge of the blade to confirm its sharpness. He slices in a motion so uniform, so controlled, and so smooth that it seems barely human. Finally, he gathers up the thick white noodles with the rolling pin, holds them aloft like a matador holding up the ear of a vanquished bull, bows his little automatic bow, and disappears through the indigo curtain.

Only Yoshiko and the woman with the baby are still standing on the footpath. The woman nods politely, then whispering soothingly to her baby, walks off down the street.

Yoshiko waits a moment, then bounds up the stairs to the first-floor dining room.

"Sanuki udon?" asks the waiter, using the ancient name for the prefecture of Kagawa now given to the famed local noodles, renowned for their strength and resilience.

"Sanuki udon," she confirms.

He reappears with a large bowl of noodles floating in a clear, pure dashi broth, flavored with soy and mirin. It sits on the table, steaming like the hot springs of Shionoe.

Yoshiko bends over the bowl as if praying. Her slight body moves with the rhythm of her breath.

She then snaps her chopsticks in two, and toys playfully with the noodles, watching as they slip and slide sinuously, seemingly dancing the awa odori, the dance of joy.

She is looking at the noodles, but she is seeing his hands. Picking up a large thick udon strand, she purses her lips and begins to make a loud whooshing sound, as is traditional with the eating of hot udon. But there is something different about her whooshing—something desperate, like an injured animal gasping for breath—that makes two businessmen at the next table stop their own whooshing and stare.

She can't see them. Her eyes are shut tight as she allows the noodle to slide down, feeling his hands on her throat, feeling their two souls meet and mingle like the swirling whirlpools of the Naruta Straits.

She hurries back to work, past the empty workroom. A little light-headed still, she runs around the corner and straight into the woman with the baby, who clutches the child to her chest instinctively. The baby cries, his little hands opening and closing like oyster shells in the cold air. His hands. There are the same long fingers, the same defined knuckles, the same slight flattening around the nail. She gasps, turns, and runs.

thailand

Mee Krob	131
Gwaytio Neua Sap	132
Kao Soi	133
Khanom Jeen with Spicy Pork	134
Moo Sarong	135
Pad Thai	136
Seafood and Glass Noodle Salad	137
Pad Woon Sen	139
Thailand–Modern	
Chile Mussels with Rice Noodles	140
Glass Noodle Som Tum	141
Thai Chicken Noodle Soup	142
Beef and Glass Noodle Salad	143

Mee Krob

It doesn't matter how many times I make this dish, I'm like a child gazing in wonder when the noodles puff up in the oil. In Thailand, the ingredients for mee krob vary according to what's in season and what's on hand, so feel free to improvise a little. This is a big favorite at parties.

Peanut oil, for deep-frying
4 ounces rice vermicelli
6 shallots, finely chopped
4 cloves garlic, finely chopped
5 ounces pork loin, finely chopped
5 ounces chicken breast, finely chopped
5 ounces peeled shrimp, finely chopped
4 ounces firm tofu, diced
1 small red chile, thinly sliced
2 tablespoons palm sugar
2 tablespoons fish sauce (nam pla)
2 tablespoons vinegar
Juice of 1 lime
3 ounces bean sprouts

To Serve:
3 fresh red chiles, sliced
½ cup loosely packed cilantro leaves
3 green onions, finely chopped

Heat oil in a hot wok until almost smoking. Cut noodles into manageable lengths with a pair of scissors and deep-fry a handful at a time. When noodles puff up and turn golden (a matter of seconds), remove and drain on paper towels.

Pour off all but 1 tablespoon oil. Fry shallots and garlic until they start to brown. Add pork, chicken, shrimp, tofu, and chile and lightly stir-fry for 3 minutes, until meat is cooked. Add sugar, fish sauce, and vinegar and cook, stirring, for 30 seconds.

Add lime juice, bean sprouts, and noodles and toss quickly, then immediately bring to the table before mixture softens. Scatter with chiles, cilantro leaves, and green onions. Serve with forks and spoons.

For a more dramatic effect, put crisp noodles on a large serving plate. Pour the sauce over, and scatter with chiles, bean sprouts, cilantro leaves, and green onions. Top with more crisp noodles. Bring to the table and toss.

Serves 4

noodle ID 8

Gwaytio Neua Sap

Thai people are particularly fond of fresh rice noodles and incorporate them into a number of truly original dishes. Yet for some strange reason, very few of these dishes ever seem to make it out of Thailand. Unusually gentle in its spicing, this homey noodle dish lets the textures do the talking, playing off the soft silky feel of the noodle against the crisp crunch of lettuce leaves and bean sprouts.

1 pound fresh rice sheet noodles, cut into ½-inch strips
4 tablespoons peanut oil
1 tablespoon dark soy sauce
6 lettuce leaves, coarsely torn
3 shallots, finely chopped
2 cloves garlic, finely chopped
7 ounces finely ground beef
3 ounces bean sprouts, blanched briefly in boiling water and rinsed in cold
¾ cup chicken stock
1 tablespoon light soy sauce
1 tablespoon fish sauce (nam pla)
1 tablespoon preserved shredded Thai radish
1 teaspoon cornstarch, mixed with a little cold water
1 green onion, thinly sliced
1 small bunch cilantro leaves, coarsely chopped

Pour boiling water over noodles in a bowl and carefully separate noodles with chopsticks. Drain as quickly as possible.

Heat 2 tablespoons of oil in a hot wok and stir-fry noodles with dark soy sauce for 1 minute. Arrange lettuce on a serving plate and tip noodles out onto the bed of lettuce.

Brown shallots in 2 tablespoons oil, adding garlic toward the end of browning time. Add beef and cook over high heat until browned. Reduce heat and add bean sprouts, stock, light soy sauce, fish sauce, and preserved radish. When sauce begins to boil, add cornstarch mixture and stir well until thickened. Transfer to a saucepan and keep warm.

Pour sauce over noodles. Scatter with green onion and cilantro, and serve with forks and spoons.

Serves 4

noodle ID 7

Kao Soi

Also known as Chiang Mai noodles, this northern Thai dish of curried noodles with its crackling topping of crisp, deep-fried noodles has been called the Thai answer to Malaysian laksa. Yet kao soi, which shows heavy Burmese influences, has a complexity and character all its own.

Vegetable oil, for deep-frying
14 ounces fresh egg noodles
3 chicken leg and thigh portions
2½ cups coconut milk
2 tablespoons Thai red curry paste (see Basics, page 191)
½ teaspoon ground turmeric
½ teaspoon ground cumin
2½ cups chicken stock
1 tablespoon fish sauce (nam pla)
1 teaspoon sugar
1 teaspoon salt
2 green onions, green part only, thinly sliced
3 tablespoons coarsely chopped cilantro
2 limes, halved

To Serve:
½ cup Thai pickled mustard cabbage
4 shallots, thinly sliced
1 tablespoon crushed red pepper flakes

Heat oil in a hot wok and deep-fry a quarter of the noodles until crisp and golden, about 1 minute. Drain on paper towels. Cook remaining noodles in boiling water for a minute. Rinse with cold water, drain, and set aside.

Chop chicken portions across the bone into about 1-inch pieces. In a clean wok, heat 1 cup of the thicker coconut cream that has risen to the surface of the milk, add red curry paste, turmeric, and cumin and fry until the fragrant aroma tells you it's ready, about 2 to 3 minutes. Add chicken and stir-fry for 2 minutes. Add remaining coconut milk, stock, fish sauce, sugar, and salt and simmer, stirring, for 15 minutes, until chicken is cooked through.

Rinse the boiled noodles in boiling water to heat. Drain and divide among 4 large soup bowls. Ladle soup into bowls and top with fried noodles, green onions, and cilantro. Place half a lime in each bowl and serve with separate bowls of Thai pickled mustard cabbage, shallots, and crushed red pepper flakes. Serve with forks and spoons.

Serves 4

noodle ID 2

Pad Thai

When people refer to "Thai noodles," they usually mean pad Thai. Jumping with flavor and dead easy to make, this is a dish that's equally at home at a dinner party, in a street hawker's wok, or on the finest china of an upscale restaurant.

6 ounces rice sticks
¼ cup peanut oil
2 shallots, chopped
2 cloves garlic, finely chopped
2 eggs, beaten
7 ounces small shrimp, cooked and peeled
1 cup bean sprouts
2 green onions, cut into 1-inch pieces
2 tablespoons fish sauce (nam pla)
2 tablespoons chopped roasted peanuts
2 tablespoons dried shrimp, ground to a powder
1 tablespoon ketchup
1 tablespoon freshly squeezed lime juice
1 tablespoon preserved shredded Thai radish
1 teaspoon sugar
1 dried chile, ground to a powder
2 tablespoons chopped cilantro
1 lime, cut in wedges

Soak noodles in hot water for about 15 minutes, or until soft. Rinse in cold water and drain.

Heat oil in a hot wok and cook shallots for a few minutes, until golden. Add garlic and cook for 1 minute, taking care not to let it burn. Add beaten eggs, allow to set for a minute or two, then stir with a spoon to scramble lightly. Add drained noodles, tossing well to combine with the egg. Add shrimp, 1/2 cup bean sprouts, green onions, fish sauce, 1 tablespoon peanuts, 1 tablespoon shrimp powder, ketchup, lime juice, preserved radish, sugar, and chile powder. Stir constantly until heated through.

Transfer to a serving dish and sprinkle with remaining shrimp powder, peanuts, bean sprouts, and the cilantro. Add a lime wedge or 2 to each plate. Serve with forks and spoons.

Serves 4

Seafood and Glass Noodle Salad

The real secret of this wonderfully refreshing summer salad is the dried shrimp powder, which imbues the whole thing with what I can only describe as an enchanting Thai accent. It's a good idea to keep a small electric coffee grinder just for grinding your spices, but never use the one you use for your coffee beans. A touch of the button, and you have instant shrimp powder.

5 ounces bean thread vermicelli
5 ounces squid tubes, cleaned
1 tablespoon peanut oil
5 ounces small shrimp, peeled and deveined
2 cloves garlic, finely chopped
2 tablespoons peanuts, coarsely chopped
2 tablespoons fish sauce (nam pla)
2 green onions, green part only, sliced
2 tablespoons chopped cilantro
2 tablespoons freshly squeezed lime juice
2 red chiles, chopped
2 tablespoons dried shrimp powder

Pour boiling water over noodles and let stand for 3 to 5 minutes. Drain and rinse under cold water. Drain again.

Cut squid tubes into about 1-inch squares, and score the underside in a criss-cross pattern with the tip of a sharp knife.

Heat oil in a hot wok and quickly stir-fry squid and shrimp until shrimp just changes color, a little more than 1 minute.

Combine noodles and seafood in a bowl with the garlic, peanuts, fish sauce, green onions, cilantro, lime juice, chiles, and shrimp powder. Serve warm or at room temperature with forks and spoons.

Serves 4

noodle ID 11

Pad Woon Sen

Always a dramatic dish to make because of the appealing see-through nature of the cellophane noodles, this quick and easy stir-fry is a popular lunchtime snack throughout Thailand. If the noodles start getting hard to handle, a few snips here and there with a pair of scissors will cut them down to size.

7 ounces bean thread vermicelli
3 tablespoons vegetable oil
3 cloves garlic, finely chopped
3 ounces lean pork, thinly sliced
5 ounces small shrimp, peeled and deveined
2 stalks celery with leaves, finely chopped
3 ounces bean sprouts, lightly blanched
2 tablespoons fish sauce (nam pla)
2 tablespoons light soy sauce
2 tablespoons chicken stock
1 teaspoon sugar
Ground white pepper, to taste
2 tablespoons cilantro
4 tablespoons roasted peanuts, coarsely crushed
1 lime, quartered

Pour boiling water over noodles and soak for 3 to 5 minutes. Drain.

Heat oil in a hot wok and fry garlic until golden. Add pork and stir-fry until meat is opaque. Add shrimp and stir-fry for 1 minute. Add noodles and toss lightly.

Add celery, bean sprouts, fish sauce, soy sauce, chicken stock, sugar, and white pepper. Heat through and serve on a large platter or in small Asian bowls. Scatter with cilantro and peanuts and serve with lime wedges. Serve with forks and spoons.

Serves 4

noodle ID 11

Chile Mussels with Rice Noodles

Mussels (or clams if you prefer) take on a luscious, seductive character when powered by the dense fiery tang of Thai chile paste. Traditionally, this dish would be served with rice, but rice noodles are equally compatible. Fresh rice ribbon noodles would work just as well.

3 pounds mussels
3 tablespoons peanut oil
3 cloves garlic, chopped
3 red chiles, finely chopped
1 tablespoon grated ginger
½ cup dry white wine
13 ounces fresh round rice noodles (khanom jeen) or thin Vietnamese bun noodles
2 tablespoons fish sauce (nam pla)
1 tablespoon Thai chile paste (jam) or sweet chile sauce
1 tablespoon lime juice
Small bunch cilantro, coarsely chopped
1 lime, quartered

Remove beards from mussels and lightly scrub the shells.

In a heavy-bottomed pan, heat oil and stir-fry garlic, chiles, and ginger for 1 minute. Add white wine and turn up the heat. Add mussels and cook, covered, for 1 to 2 minutes on high heat. Remove lid and use kitchen tongs to take out any mussels that have opened. Cover for another 30 seconds, remove lid, and take out any more mussels that have opened. Continue this process another two or three times. Discard any mussels that do not open.

Place noodles in a bowl and cover with boiling water. Gently separate noodles with chopsticks, taking care not to break or damage them. Drain well, arrange noodles on a large serving platter, and put mussels on top.

Add fish sauce, chile paste, and lime juice to the cooking juices and bring to a boil, stirring. Taste and adjust flavors accordingly. Pour over mussels and noodles, scatter with cilantro and lime wedges, and serve.

Serves 4

noodle ID 9

Glass Noodle Som Tum

With its delectable crunch and sassy sweet-and-sour flavors, there is absolutely nothing wrong with the traditional som tum green papaya salad just as it is. But when I see a perfect noodle opportunity just waiting to be snapped up, I can't help myself.

7 ounces bean thread vermicelli
½ green (unripe) papaya
6 green beans
2 ripe tomatoes
4 shallots, very thinly sliced
1 clove garlic, crushed with the side of a knife blade
1 red chile
1 tablespoon dried shrimp
1 tablespoon palm sugar
3 tablespoons mint leaves
2 tablespoons lime juice
2 tablespoons fish sauce (nam pla)
2 tablespoons crushed roasted peanuts

Soak noodles in boiling water for 3 to 5 minutes. Rinse in cold water, drain well, and set aside.

Peel papaya and remove seeds. Thinly slice flesh, then cut each slice into thin matchsticks. Drain, rinse in cold water, and set aside. Cut beans into fine matchsticks and cook in simmering, salted water for 30 seconds. Drain, rinse under cold water, and set aside. Cut the thick outer flesh from tomatoes and discard the rest. Slice tomato into slivers.

Pound or blend the shallots, garlic, and chile until mushy. Add shrimp and palm sugar and continue to pound to a rough paste. Add beans, tomato, and mint leaves and toss. Add lime juice and fish sauce. Add papaya and noodles and toss lightly. Pile high on a serving platter and scatter with crushed peanuts.

Serves 4 as a salad

Thai Chicken Noodle Soup

Tom kha gai, *creamy, coconutty, galangal-powered chicken soup, is second only to the great* tom yam goong *in Thailand's chart-topping soups. By adding rice noodles, you get an effect not unlike a Thai curry laksa.*

2 stalks lemongrass, white part only
14 ounces boneless chicken
4 cups coconut milk
1 cup chicken stock
4 kaffir lime leaves
5 slices galangal
2 tablespoons fish sauce (nam pla)
1 teaspoon sugar
½ teaspoon salt
2 small red chiles
2 tablespoons lime juice
10 ounces fresh round rice noodles (khanom jeen) or cooked rice vermicelli
3 tablespoons cilantro

Bruise lemongrass and cut into 1-inch pieces. Cut chicken into bite-size pieces. Bring half the coconut milk and chicken stock to a boil, and add chicken, lemongrass, lime leaves, galangal, 1 tablespoon fish sauce, sugar, and salt. Simmer for 15 minutes. Stir in remaining coconut milk. Toss in chiles and add remaining tablespoon fish sauce and lime juice. Remove from the heat.

Put noodles in a bowl and cover with boiling water. Separate gently with chopsticks, then drain well and distribute among 4 deep soup bowls. Ladle soup and chicken over the noodles and sprinkle cilantro on top. Serve with forks and spoons.

Serves 4

noodle ID 9

Beef and Glass Noodle Salad

Another Thai classic (yam neua or rare-beef salad) gets the noodle treatment and is transformed into something thoroughly wonderful. The glossy, slippery noodles not only add texture and interest, but also tend to lighten the dish, taking a little of the heaviness away from the meat.

8 ounces bean thread vermicelli
1 tablespoon jasmine rice
3 dried chiles
14 ounces beef sirloin or tenderloin steak
6 shallots, thinly sliced
3 green onions, thinly sliced
3 tablespoons lime juice
3 tablespoons fish sauce (nam pla)
1 teaspoon sugar
1 cup lightly packed mint leaves
1 cup lightly packed Thai basil or cilantro

Pour boiling water over noodles in a bowl and let stand for 3 to 5 minutes. Rinse in cold water and drain well. With a pair of scissors, roughly cut the noodles so they are a manageable length, and set aside.

Toast rice in a dry, heavy-bottomed frying pan until lightly golden. Grind or pound rice to a powder and set aside.

Toast dried chiles in the same pan until quite smoky, then grind to a powder and set aside.

Grill or broil steak quickly so it is still quite rare and let rest for about 15 minutes.

Mix 1 teaspoon of the chile powder with rice powder, shallots, green onions, lime juice, fish sauce, and sugar in a large bowl. Slice beef thinly and add it to the mixture, along with the noodles, mint, and Thai basil. Toss lightly and serve piled high on a large platter.

Serves 4

noodle ID 11

Thailand—Modern   143

vietnam

Bun Rieu Noodle Soup with Crab Dumplings	147
Bun Bo Hué	148
Cellophane Noodles with Shrimp	149
Cha Gio (Finger-Size Spring Rolls)	150
Goi Cuon (Fresh Spring Rolls)	151
Pho Bo	152
Pho Ga	153
Nem Nuong	155

Bun Rieu Noodle Soup with Crab Dumplings

This intriguingly aromatic noodle and crab dumpling soup is usually made with the small, freshwater crabs found in the rice paddies. If you don't happen to have a rice paddy nearby, any crab will do, as long as it's fresh.

4 ounces ground pork
3 tablespoons dried shrimp, soaked in hot water for 30 minutes
7 ounces crabmeat
1 teaspoon shrimp paste
Pinch of salt
Pinch of pepper
1 small egg, lightly beaten
2 tablespoons peanut oil
4 shallots, thinly sliced
2 cloves garlic, finely chopped
2 red chiles, sliced
3 tomatoes, cut into wedges
8 cups chicken stock
2 tablespoons fish sauce (nuoc mam)
1 tablespoon white rice vinegar
½ teaspoon sugar
13 ounces thin fresh round rice noodles (bun)
1 cup bean sprouts
2 green onions, thinly sliced
1 bunch ngo gai (saw-leaf plant) or cilantro
2 limes, cut into wedges
Leaves from 1 small bunch mint

Using a food processor or mortar and pestle, blend pork, drained shrimp, and half the crabmeat until it forms a smooth paste. Transfer to a bowl and mix in shrimp paste, salt, pepper, and remaining crab by hand. Beat in egg with a fork and refrigerate dumpling mixture for an hour.

Heat oil in a saucepan and cook shallots for 2 to 3 minutes. Add garlic and half the red chiles and cook for another 30 seconds. Add tomatoes and cook for 1 minute. Add stock, fish sauce, vinegar, and sugar. Bring soup to a simmer.

Shape 1 tablespoon of dumpling mixture into a football shape and gently add it to the boiling stock. Repeat until all the dumpling mixture is used. Cover and simmer for 4 minutes, or until dumplings are firm and floating.

Pour boiling water over noodles in a bowl. Gently shake loose with chopsticks, drain, and divide among 4 soup bowls. Top with bean sprouts, green onions, dumplings, and soup. Serve with a bowl of ngo gai or cilantro leaves, lime wedges, mint leaves, and remaining chile to be added according to individual taste.

Serves 4

noodle ID 9

Cha Gio (Finger-Size Spring Rolls)

What makes this dish special is the way it is eaten. The crisp, deep-fried rolls are wrapped with fresh herbs and lettuce leaves, then dipped in sweet/sour/spicy nuoc cham *sauce. Textures and flavors run around the mouth like excited schoolchildren.*

2 ounces bean thread vermicelli
7 ounces ground chicken
7 ounces ground pork
3 ounces crabmeat
3 ounces shrimp, peeled, deveined, and finely chopped
Tablespoon dried wood ear mushrooms ($^1/_8$ ounce), soaked in hot water for 1 hour and shredded
4 shallots, finely chopped
2 cloves garlic, finely chopped
1 tablespoon fish sauce (nuoc mam)
½ teaspoon white pepper
4 cups warm water
1 tablespoon white rice vinegar
1 tablespoon sugar
30 small rounds rice paper (banh trang)
1 tablespoon cornstarch mixed with 1 tablespoon cold water
Peanut oil, for deep-frying
Leaves from iceberg lettuce, large leaves torn in half
1 bunch Thai basil or common basil
1 bunch Vietnamese mint (rau ram) or common mint
1 quantity nuoc cham (see Basics, page 192)

Soak noodles in boiling water for 3 to 4 minutes, rinse in cold water, drain, and cut into about 2½-inch lengths. In a bowl, combine chicken, pork, crab, shrimp, mushrooms, noodles, shallots, garlic, fish sauce, and pepper.

Combine warm water with vinegar and sugar in a wide, shallow bowl or frying pan and soak a rice paper until it becomes soft and pliable. Remove to a dry dish towel and repeat the process with remaining rice papers.

Take a softened paper and put a tablespoon of filling just above the center. Bring the top edge of the paper down over the filling and roll it over itself once. Tuck in both ends and continue rolling tightly until it resembles a thin cigar about 3 inches long. Moisten the bottom of the rice paper with a little cornstarch paste and press to seal. Repeat with remaining wrappers and filling.

Pour enough oil for deep-frying into a hot wok and heat until a cube of bread dances on the surface. Cook the rolls, a few at a time, for about 8 minutes, or until they are lightly golden and cooked through.

To eat, wrap each roll in a lettuce leaf, tucking in basil and mint along the way. Serve with nuoc cham for dipping.

Serves 4

noodle ID 11

Goi Cuon (Fresh Spring Rolls)

Fresh spring rolls are currently riding the crest of the fusion popularity wave. Inventive chefs all over the world are stuffing them with all manner of weird and not-always-wonderful things. The real secret, however, is to keep the filling fresh and relatively simple. The other secret is to eat them as soon as they are made.

3 ounces rice vermicelli
8 large rounds dried rice paper (banh trang)
1 cup shredded iceberg lettuce
¼ cup fresh bean sprouts
¼ cup peanuts, coarsely chopped
Leaves from 1 bunch of mint
Leaves from 1 bunch of cilantro
16 small shrimp, cooked and peeled
16 flat garlic chives
1 quantity nuoc cham (see Basics, page 192)

Pour boiling water over noodles in a bowl and leave for 6 to 7 minutes. Drain, then transfer to a saucepan of boiling water and cook for 1 more minute. Rinse in cold water and drain again.

Dunk each rice paper round in warm water for a few seconds until soft. Spread out to drain on serving plates.

On each paper put some shredded lettuce, noodles, bean sprouts, peanuts, mint, and cilantro, and fold the rice paper toward the center to form a firm roll. Tuck in 2 shrimp, fold in ends of rice paper, and put 2 garlic chives in the crease so they protrude by about 1 inch. Roll into a neat sausage shape. The rice paper will stick to itself and hold the shape. Serve with nuoc cham for dipping.

Serves 4

noodle ID 8

Pho Bo

What began life as an honest laborer's breakfast dish of noodle soup laced with beefy bits has gone on to hijack lunchtimes all over the world.

2 pounds beef bones
4 quarts water
2 onions, quartered, plus 1 onion, very thinly sliced
1 teaspoon salt
2 knobs ginger, about 1 inch round
5 cardamom pods
3 star anise
1 cinnamon stick
1 pound beef brisket
2 tablespoons fish sauce (nuoc mam)
1 pound fresh rice sheet noodles
8 ounces beef tenderloin or sirloin, sliced paper-thin
4 green onions, finely chopped
White pepper for sprinkling

Accompaniments:
Fish sauce (nuoc mam)
Hoisin sauce (optional)
2 limes, cut into wedges
3 small fresh chiles, chopped
A few sprigs each of Asian basil, cilantro, and Vietnamese mint (rau ram)
2 cups bean sprouts, washed

Put bones in a large saucepan with the water, 1 quartered onion, salt, 1 knob ginger, cardamom pods, star anise, and cinnamon. Grill or broil remaining quartered onion and ginger until skins are burnt, add them to the stock, and bring to a boil. Skim off any froth that rises, add the brisket, bring to a boil, and skim again. Add fish sauce and simmer for 4 hours.

Remove brisket and slice half of it very thinly. Strain stock into a jug or saucepan.

Cut rice noodles into ½-inch strips and put in a large bowl. Cover with boiling water and soak for 20 seconds, gently separating noodles with a pair of chopsticks. Drain and divide noodles among 6 bowls. Top with 3 or 4 slices of brisket and raw steak. Then add a few onion slices and some green onion.

Bring soup to a boil, ladle over meat and noodles, and sprinkle with pepper. If desired, flavor with extra fish sauce or hoisin sauce to taste. Serve with any or all of the accompaniments listed to add as you wish.

Serves 6

noodle ID 7

Pho Ga

The real, the true, the original pho *(pronounced somewhere between "far" and "fer") is* pho bo. *Yet this chicken version is every bit as satisfying and complex, albeit lighter, sweeter, and a touch more subtle.*

12 cups water
1 whole chicken, about 3 pounds, preferably with head and feet
2 pounds chicken bones
2 onions, thinly sliced
2-inch knob ginger, peeled and sliced
1 cinnamon stick
1 star anise
3 cardamom pods
1 teaspoon salt
¼ cup crisp-fried shallots (available from Asian grocery stores)
3 tablespoons fish sauce (nuoc mam)
2 teaspoons sugar
13 ounces fresh rice sheet noodles
4 green onions, thinly sliced
8 sprigs cilantro

Accompaniments:
1 cup bean sprouts
Sprigs of fresh mint
Sprigs of Thai basil
Sprigs of cilantro
1 red chile, finely chopped
1 lemon or lime, cut into wedges

Combine water, whole chicken, chicken bones, 1 sliced onion, ginger, cinnamon, star anise, cardamom pods, and salt in a large pot and bring to a boil. Skim off any froth that rises to the surface, lower heat, and simmer for 1½ hours, until chicken is fully cooked. Remove whole chicken and reserve.

Add 2 tablespoons crisp-fried shallots, fish sauce, and sugar to stock and cook for another hour. Strain stock through a fine sieve.

Remove meat from chicken thigh and breast and thinly slice.

Cut rice noodles (if not precut) into ½-inch strips. Put in a bowl, cover with boiling water, shake gently apart with chopsticks, and drain.

To assemble soup, divide rice noodles among 4 deep soup bowls. Layer sliced chicken meat neatly on top and spoon hot soup into each bowl. Scatter remaining crisp-fried shallots, green onions, and cilantro on top.

Serve with an accompanying platter of bean sprouts, mint, basil, cilantro, chile, and lemon or lime wedges for each person to add according to their taste.

Serves 4

noodle ID 7

Nem Nuong

The Vietnamese have a happy knack of turning practically any grilled meat into a complete meal just by serving it on a bed of rice noodles and accompanying it with a bowl of nuoc cham. *Rarely, however, does the idea work as well as it does with these moist, delicious pork meatballs served on a bed of rice vermicelli.*

1 tablespoon jasmine rice
1 pound boneless pork shoulder or neck
2 tablespoons sugar
2 tablespoons fish sauce (nuoc mam)
3 cloves garlic, finely chopped
¼ teaspoon white pepper
3 ounces pork fat, chopped into small cubes
1 teaspoon salt
Pinch of baking powder
8 ounces rice vermicelli
1 cup loosely packed bean sprouts
1 small cucumber, peeled and sliced
½ cup peanuts, coarsely chopped
Leaves from 1 small bunch Thai basil or common mint
1 quantity nuoc cham (see Basics, page 192)

Toast rice in a dry, heavy-bottomed frying pan until lightly golden. Grind or pound rice to a coarse powder and set aside. Soak 8 wooden skewers in cold water for 1 hour to help prevent them from burning on the grill.

Cut pork into thin strips and mix with sugar, fish sauce, garlic, and pepper. Cover and let stand for 30 minutes.

Transfer meat to a food processor with pork fat, ground roasted rice, and salt and purée until it is a pale, smooth paste. Mix in baking powder with your hands and, using hands again, roll mixture into balls the size of small plums. Thread balls onto wooden skewers and grill until well browned and cooked through.

Meanwhile, cover noodles in boiling water and leave for 6 to 7 minutes. Drain, then transfer to a saucepan of boiling water and cook for 1 more minute. Rinse with cold water and drain. Put a little vermicelli on 4 plates and top with the meatballs. On a separate plate, arrange bean sprouts, cucumber, peanuts, and basil to pass separately. The meatballs can also be wrapped in rice paper rounds and lettuce leaves at the table. Serve with nuoc cham for dipping.

Serves 4

Chap Chae

Normal Chinese bean thread noodles will work well in this much-loved noodle, beef, and vegetable stir-fry, but it's worth sniffing out a Korean food store for genuine dang myun. The extra body and extra chew in these Korean potato starch noodles give the dish much more body and presence.

7 ounces dang myun potato starch noodles or bean thread vermicelli
13 ounces tenderloin or sirloin beef, cut into thick matchstick strips
4 tablespoons dark soy sauce
4 cloves garlic, finely chopped
2 green onions, thinly sliced
1 tablespoon sesame seeds, lightly toasted in a dry pan
2 teaspoons sesame oil
2 teaspoons sugar
2 dried shiitake mushrooms
5 tablespoons peanut oil
2 eggs, lightly beaten
½ carrot, cut into matchsticks
1 onion, cut into thin matchsticks
1 cup loosely packed bean sprouts
¼ Peking cabbage, shredded
1 small cucumber, cut into matchsticks
½ cup fresh wood ear mushrooms, or 4 abalone or oyster mushrooms, cut into strips
Salt to taste
Pinch of ground dried chile
1 tablespoon pine nuts

Boil noodles in plenty of water for 3 minutes. Rinse in cold water, drain, and cut into 5-inch lengths. Combine beef, 2 tablespoons soy sauce, garlic, green onions, sesame seeds, 1 teaspoon sesame oil, and 1 teaspoon sugar, and marinate for an hour.

Soak shiitake mushrooms in hot water for 1 hour. Drain, discard stems, and cut caps into fine strips. Using 1 tablespoon of peanut oil and the beaten eggs, make omelet according to directions on page 190.

Heat 2 tablespoons peanut oil in a hot wok and cook carrot and onion until they soften. Add bean sprouts and cabbage and stir-fry for 2 minutes. Stir cucumber through mixture and set aside.

Heat remaining 2 tablespoons peanut oil in a hot wok and stir-fry beef and mushrooms for 2 minutes. Add noodles, remaining 2 tablespoons soy sauce, 1 teaspoon each sugar and sesame oil, a pinch of salt, and chile. Stir in vegetables and pine nuts, and heat through, stirring, for 3 minutes. Serve on a large platter, topped with omelet strips. Serve with chopsticks.

Serves 4

noodle ID 19

Bibim Naeng Myun

Crisp is not a word that usually springs to mind when you talk about boiled noodles, but this Korean favorite is lifted considerably by a veritable chorus line of in-your-face crunches. The addition of cucumber, daikon, and nashi pear also gives the dish a curiously pleasing flavor twist.

10 ounces naeng myun noodles
2 tablespoons sesame oil
2 cloves garlic, finely chopped
¼ cup gochu jang chile paste (from Korean or Japanese grocery stores)
¼ cup Korean beef broth (see Basics, page 193)
2 tablespoons soy sauce
2 tablespoons sugar
1 teaspoon sesame seeds
1 small cucumber
½ teaspoon salt
1 nashi pear
3 ounces Korean daikon pickles (see Basics, page 193)
16 slices cooked beef (from beef broth, above)
2 green onions, green part only, thinly sliced
2 hard-boiled eggs, halved

Cook noodles in boiling water for 4 to 5 minutes. Rinse under cold water and drain. Toss with 1 tablespoon sesame oil, cover, and refrigerate.

To make sauce, mix garlic, chile paste, remaining sesame oil, beef broth, soy sauce, sugar, and sesame seeds together. Peel cucumber, cut in half lengthwise, and discard seeds. Cut into thin slices, sprinkle with salt, and leave to sweat for 10 minutes, then drain and dry with paper towels. Peel pear and cut into matchsticks about 2½ inches long.

Divide noodles among 4 large soup bowls. Arrange the cucumber, pear, daikon pickle, beef slices, green onions, and hard-boiled egg on top of the noodles.

Divide sauce among 4 small bowls and give one to each person to use as little or as much as desired. The sauce is added to the noodles, then the whole thing is tossed before eating. Serve at room temperature with chopsticks.

Serves 4

noodle ID 18

Kalgooksu

Koreans have a gift for getting beef into practically every dish they cook. This combination of beef strips with a highly flavored anchovy stock may seem odd at first, but the end result is surprisingly soothing and even tastes vaguely familiar.

8 ounces beef sirloin or rump steak
3 tablespoons soy sauce
2 red chiles, thinly sliced
2 tablespoons toasted sesame seeds
1 tablespoon sesame oil
3 cloves garlic, crushed with the side of a knife blade
3 green onions, thinly sliced, keeping green and white parts separate
½ teaspoon ground cayenne pepper
¼ teaspoon black pepper
8 cups water
20 dried anchovies (from Korean or Japanese grocery stores)
1 small carrot, cut into thin matchsticks
13 ounces dried round gooksu white wheat noodles
2 small zucchini, cut into matchsticks
1 pound clams, scrubbed
¼ cup white wine
1 tablespoon peanut oil

Cut beef into strips 1 inch long and ½ inch thick. Combine with 2 tablespoons soy sauce, chiles, sesame seeds, sesame oil, garlic, half the green onion greens, cayenne, and black pepper. Cover and let stand for 20 minutes.

Bring water to a boil. Add anchovies and simmer for 10 minutes. Scoop out and discard anchovies. Add 1 tablespoon soy sauce, carrot, white parts of green onions, and noodles and simmer for 4 minutes. Add zucchini and cook for another 3 minutes.

Meanwhile, put clams and white wine in a saucepan, cover, and steam over high heat until clams open. Remove clams and set aside. Strain broth through cheesecloth and add it to the anchovy stock.

Heat peanut oil in a hot wok, add beef mixture, and stir-fry for 2 minutes. Divide noodles among 4 serving bowls and pour stock and vegetables over. In neat little clumps on top, add a few clams, a little nest of beef strips, and a pile of the remaining green onion greens. Serve with chopsticks and spoons.

Serves 4

Mandu Kuk

Mandu are beef dumplings that bear more than a passing resemblance to Japanese gyoza *or the Chinese* wor tip. *They can be pan-fried or deep-fried, but are at their best when boiled and served in soup. If you don't feel like making them yourself, you can buy ready-made frozen dumplings from Korean and Japanese grocery stores. The addition of dang myun noodles turns the whole thing into a kind of wonton noodle soup with attitude.*

3 ounces dang myun noodles
8 cups Korean beef broth (see Basics, page 193)
8 ounces ground beef
1 small onion, finely chopped
4 cloves garlic, finely chopped
3 tablespoons soy sauce
1 tablespoon sesame oil
1 cup bean sprouts, blanched
12 mandu dumplings (see Basics, page 192), cooked
3 green onions, green parts only, thinly sliced

Put noodles in boiling water and cook for 3 minutes. Rinse well in cold water and drain thoroughly. Set aside until needed.

Heat beef broth until simmering. Heat a dry wok, add beef, onion, garlic, soy sauce, and sesame oil, and stir-fry until meat is cooked. Add mixture to the beef broth and simmer for 10 minutes. Add noodles, bean sprouts, and dumplings and cook for another minute or two until dumplings are warmed through. Divide among 4 bowls and scatter with green onions. Serve with chopsticks and spoons.

Serves 4

Mu Chungol

Yet another variation on beef and noodle soup, but one with a gentle, homey, unassuming quality more suited to a family dinner than a restaurant. If Koreans ever attempted to make minestrone, the end result would probably look like this.

2 eggs
2 tablespoons peanut oil
1 onion, cut lengthwise into slivers
7 ounces daikon (white radish), cut into matchsticks
1 small zucchini, cut into matchsticks
7 ounces beef rump or sirloin steak, cut into matchsticks
8 cups Korean beef broth (see Basics, page 193)
2 teaspoons sesame oil
½ teaspoon salt
Pinch of pepper
2 cakes (3½ ounces) fresh tofu, cut into small cubes
2 green onions, cut into 2-inch slivers
5 ounces dang myun noodles

Beat eggs lightly. Heat 1 tablespoon peanut oil in a hot wok and swirl around to coat surface. Pour in beaten eggs and quickly swirl around the pan to form a thin omelet. When cooked on one side, gently separate the edge of the omelet from the wok with a knife. Place a plate over the wok and invert the whole thing so that the omelet drops onto the plate. Slide the omelet back in and quickly cook the other side. Flip omelet onto cutting board, roll up into a tight roll, slice across into thin strips, and set aside.

In a large saucepan, heat remaining peanut oil and fry onion for 2 minutes. Add daikon and zucchini and fry for another 2 minutes. Add beef and fry for 1 minute. Pour in broth, and season with sesame oil, salt, and pepper. Add tofu and simmer for 5 to 6 minutes, carefully skimming off any froth that rises to the surface. Add green onions during the last minute.

Meanwhile, cook noodles in boiling water for about 3 minutes. Drain and cut up with a few snips of kitchen scissors. Divide among 4 large soup bowls. Pour soup, beef, and vegetables over noodles. Sprinkle with omelet strips and serve with chopsticks and spoons.

Serves 4

noodle ID 19

Mul Naeng Myun

This popular Korean dish owes a lot to chilled Japanese buckwheat noodle dishes, such as zaru soba and, indeed, soba noodles can be substituted here. One of the real joys about eating this dish in Korea is the meticulous and eye-catching arrangement of the ingredients on top of the noodles, practically an art form in its own right.

10 ounces naeng myun (buckwheat and potato starch) noodles or soba noodles
8 cups Korean beef broth (see Basics, page 193), chilled
2 long green chiles, cut into thin strips
½ quantity Korean daikon pickles (see Basics, page 193)
½ quantity Korean cucumber pickles (see Basics, page 193)
24 thin slices cooked beef (from beef used to make the stock)
2 hard-boiled eggs, halved
1 teaspoon crushed red pepper flakes

Accompaniments:
Hot mustard
vinegar
soy sauce

Cook noodles in a pot of simmering water for about 3 to 4 minutes, until tender, rinse thoroughly in cold water, drain, and chill.

When cold, divide noodles among 4 large, shallow bowls. Pour 1 to 2 cups of cold broth over each serving and carefully arrange strips of chile, daikon pickles, and cucumber pickles in neat little bundles on top of the noodles.

Fan out 6 slices of meat on top, and top with half a hard-boiled egg and sprinkled crushed red pepper flakes.

Serve with hot mustard, vinegar, and soy sauce. Serve with chopsticks and spoons.

Serves 4

noodle ID 18

Spicy Squid with Somen

Somen noodles are almost as popular in Korea as they are in Japan, but while the Japanese generally prefer to eat their somen cold with a subtle dipping sauce, the Koreans are far more adventurous and often throw them into powerful, almost rustic dishes such as this spicy stir-fry.

5 ounces somen noodles
1 pound squid, cleaned
2 tablespoons peanut oil
2 teaspoons grated ginger
2 cloves garlic, finely chopped
1 small carrot, cut into thin matchsticks
1 onion, cut into lengthwise slivers
2 green onions, thinly sliced
1 teaspoon sugar
¼ teaspoon salt
1 tablespoon gochu jang chile paste (from Korean or Japanese grocery stores)
1 teaspoon sesame oil
1 teaspoon toasted sesame seeds

Cook noodles for about 1 minute in a pot of boiling water. Drain and set aside.

Cut squid into strips about ½ inch wide and 2 inches long.

Heat peanut oil in a hot wok and stir-fry ginger and garlic for 30 seconds. Add carrot and onion and stir-fry for 4 minutes. Add squid, green onions, sugar, and salt and stir-fry for another minute.

Mix in chile paste, sesame oil, and sesame seeds. Combine stir-fry ingredients with noodles, mixing thoroughly, and serve with chopsticks.

Serves 4

noodle ID 14

Bahmi Goreng

This is the noodle equivalent of nasi goreng, or Indonesian fried rice. Like fried rice, it can accommodate whatever leftovers you have in the cupboard, so use this recipe as a guide. Indonesians like to serve it with extra kecap manis and chile sauce on the side.

10 ounces dried egg noodles
3 tablespoons peanut oil
2 eggs, beaten
1 boneless chicken breast, thinly sliced
3 ounces pork loin, thinly sliced
2 cloves garlic, crushed with the side of a knife blade
3 ounces shrimp, peeled and deveined
3 ounces Peking cabbage leaves, thinly sliced
1 stalk celery, thinly sliced
4 green onions, thinly sliced
3 tablespoons chicken stock
1 tablespoon kecap manis
1 tablespoon soy sauce
2 tablespoons crisp-fried shallots (available from Asian grocery stores)

Cook noodles in boiling water for about 4 minutes, then rinse with cold water to stop them from cooking further. Drain and set aside.

Heat 1 tablespoon of oil in a hot wok and swirl around to coat surface. Pour in beaten eggs and quickly swirl around the pan to form a thin omelet. When cooked on one side, gently separate the edge of the omelet from the wok with a knife. Place a plate over the wok and invert the whole thing so that the omelet drops onto the plate. Slide the omelet back in and quickly cook the other side. Flip omelet onto cutting board, roll up into a tight roll, slice across into thin strips, and set aside.

Heat remaining oil in the wok and stir-fry chicken, pork, and garlic until they have changed color and cooked through. Add shrimp, cabbage, celery, and green onions and toss well. Add stock, kecap manis, soy sauce, and drained noodles and mix well. Tip onto a large serving platter and scatter omelet strips and crisp-fried shallots over the top.

Serves 4

noodle ID 2

Stir-Fried Pumpkin with Rice Vermicelli

The Taiwanese love their noodles, although most of their favorites are variations of Hunanese, Sichuanese, and Shanghainese noodle dishes. Pumpkin is rarely used in noodle dishes throughout Asia. After tasting this dish, you'll wonder why.

1 pound clams, scrubbed
½ cup water
10 ounces rice vermicelli
7 ounces pumpkin, peeled
1 tablespoon peanut oil
2 green onions, thinly sliced
3 tablespoons dried shrimp, soaked for 30 minutes and drained
1 cup chicken stock
½ teaspoon sesame oil
½ teaspoon salt
½ teaspoon sugar
¼ teaspoon white pepper

To cook clams, heat water in a covered skillet until boiling. Add clams and cover tightly. Cook over high heat for 1 minute, then remove all opened clams with tongs. Cook for 1 minute more and remove all opened clams. Repeat once or twice more. Discard shells and water, and keep clams covered.

Place noodles in a bowl and cover with boiling water. Let stand for 6 to 7 minutes, then drain. Rinse under cold water, drain again, and set aside.

Cut pumpkin into fine matchsticks. Heat peanut oil in a hot wok and cook green onions and dried shrimp for 1 minute. Add pumpkin and stir-fry for another 30 seconds. Add stock and simmer for 10 minutes, or until pumpkin is tender. Add rice noodles and toss well until heated through. Add clams, sesame oil, salt, sugar, and white pepper, and serve.

Serves 4

Sevian Kheer

This sweet noodle and milk pudding is particularly popular in northern India and Pakistan, and is a favorite of Muslims, who traditionally eat it after moonrise during Ramadan. If you're lucky, you might be able to find the true sevian in an Indian food store, but traditional Italian vermicelli will also work, as long as it is very fine.

4 tablespoons ghee or clarified butter
1/3 cup cashew nuts
1/3 cup blanched almonds, coarsely chopped
1/3 cup pistachio nuts, coarsely chopped, plus extra for decoration
5 ounces sevian or thin Italian vermicelli, broken into 2-inch pieces
5 cups milk
1/3 cup golden raisins
1/2 teaspoon ground cardamom
3 tablespoons sugar
2 teaspoons rosewater
A few unsprayed rose petals, washed and dried, for decoration

Heat ghee in a heavy pan and fry cashews, almonds, and pistachios over medium heat just until they start to color.

Add noodles and fry, being careful not to let the noodles brown. As soon as they turn golden, pour in milk and bring to a simmer. Add raisins and cardamom and simmer for 15 minutes.

Add sugar and rosewater and warm through until sugar has dissolved. Serve in individual bowls, sprinkled with extra chopped pistachios and rose petals. Serve hot, or leave to cool and serve at room temperature.

Serves 4

noodle ID 6

Homemade Egg Noodles

2 cups sifted flour, more for dusting
2 eggs
3 tablespoons water
1 teaspoon corn oil or peanut oil
½ teaspoon salt

Sift flour onto a work surface and make a well in the center. Add eggs, water, oil, and salt and, with the tips of your fingers, start to draw the flour into the wet ingredients. Keep mixing, slowly tumbling the flour into the liquid until a rough, crumbly mixture is formed. Keep on working until a rough dough ball forms.

Knead dough, stretching it firmly and slapping down hard on the work surface for 5 to 10 minutes until it is smooth, lump-free, and shiny. If the dough starts to feel sticky, sprinkle a little more flour around. If it is dry and crumbly, wet your hands with water and keep working. Cover with plastic wrap and leave to rest for about 2 hours.

Cut dough in quarters. Squash the first piece down with the palm of your hand and thread it through a pasta machine on the widest setting. Sprinkle the sheet with a little flour, then thread it through again. Reduce the setting one notch and thread through twice more. When the dough sheet gets too long to handle easily, cut it in half. Keep reducing the thickness until the noodle sheet is the required thickness (thicker for Shanghai style noodles, thinner for fine egg noodles).

Feed the sheets through the cutting blade, choosing the size of noodle that's right for the dish.

Use immediately or sprinkle with flour and spread out on a tray to dry out.

Makes enough to serve 4

Homemade Udon

2 egg yolks
1½ cups water
1 tablespoon salt
7 cups sifted flour

Beat egg yolks and mix with water and salt. Put flour on a work surface, make a well in the center of the flour, and pour in the liquid. With the tips of your fingers, gradually work in the flour and slowly but steadily blend the ingredients thoroughly until they form a dough ball that holds together. Knead the dough, using all your strength, for about 10 minutes, until the dough is completely smooth with a satiny sheen to its surface. The dough should feel firm but malleable. If it is too sloppy, sprinkle with a little more flour; if it is too dry, moisten your hands with water and continue to work.

Dust a board or marble slab with flour and, using a wooden rolling pin, roll the dough out to a rectangle. Keep rolling until the dough is just less than ¼ inch thick. Sprinkle dough with flour and fold it backwards and forwards on itself three times so that the edges look like one and a half Ss. Lay the folded dough on the board and, with a very sharp knife, cut across the folds in strips, just under ¼ inch wide.

Insert a long chopstick or a piece of wooden dowel rod into the middle fold, then lift up to reveal your freshly made noodles.

Makes enough to serve 8 to 10

Homemade Soba

3²/₃ cups buckwheat flour
2²/₃ cups plain flour
2 cups water

Put the flours in a large work bowl. With a circular motion, mix them together with your hands, while at the same time adding the water, a little at a time, with the other hand. Work rapidly, blending the water and flour with your fingers. You should have poured in about three-quarters of the water in a minute. Reserve remaining water. Use the fingers and palms of both hands to feel your way through the dough, pressing it and moving it on. Grab a clump of dough in your hands, press firmly, then allow the dough clumps to fall back into the bowl. Keep working in this manner for about 3 minutes. Add remaining water and work for another minute or two.

Now it's time for some heavy kneading action. Lean heavily into the bowl, using the weight of your body, and push down on the dough, pressing it together. Keep kneading and rolling the dough until it forms a smooth ball.

Wrap dough in plastic wrap and leave to rest for an hour or two.

Cut dough in quarters. Sprinkle some buckwheat flour on a work surface and press down with the palm of your hand to flatten one dough ball a little. Using a rolling pin, roll it out to an oval about ¼ inch thick. Sprinkle some buckwheat flour over dough and cut in half. Lay both halves on top of each other, matching the cut edges, then fold them upon themselves. Starting at the flat edge, cut the dough with a sharp knife into strips ¼ inch wide. Place noodles on a tray and sprinkle with flour. Repeat with remaining dough. Noodles are now ready to cook.

Makes enough to serve 8

Sichuan Chile Oil

1 cup peanut oil
3 tablespoons crushed red pepper flakes
1 teaspoon Sichuan peppercorns

Heat oil in a wok until almost smoking, then turn off heat. Add pepper flakes and peppercorns and leave to cool. Strain through cheesecloth or a fine sieve into a screw-top bottle and store in a cool, dark place.

Chinese Chicken Stock

4½ pounds chicken bones, necks, wings, feet, etc.
7-ounce chunk of ham
2 onions, quartered
4 green onions, white part only
3 thick slices ginger

Wash bones well in cold water, then place in a pot with cold water to cover (about 12 cups). Add ham, onions, green onions, and ginger, and bring to a boil. Skim off the froth that forms on the surface, reduce heat, and simmer, partly covered, for 1 hour. Allow to cool, then strain and refrigerate.

Char Sieu (Red Roast Pork)

2½ pounds pork neck (from Asian butcher) or boneless pork loin

Marinade:
1 teaspoon salt
¼ cup soy sauce
4 slices ginger, peeled
3 tablespoons maltose (from Asian food stores) or honey, warmed
2 tablespoons white sugar
2 cloves garlic, crushed with the side of a knife blade
2 tablespoons shaohsing rice wine or dry sherry
1 teaspoon five-spice powder
2 tablespoons hoisin sauce
Drop of red food coloring or annatto powder (optional)

For Basting:
¼ cup honey, warmed

Cut pork lengthwise into 3 equal strips, roughly 1½ inches thick and 7 inches long. Combine marinade ingredients in a large bowl or pan and add pork. Leave to marinate for 6 hours, or overnight, remembering to turn the meat over every now and then.

Preheat oven to 400° F and roast pork for 20 minutes with meat lying flat on a wire rack set high in the oven. Place a roasting pan with ½ inch water underneath to catch the drips. After 20 minutes, turn pork over and brush with warmed honey. Leave for 15 minutes more, then turn and brush with honey again, and roast for a final 15 minutes. The pork should have nicely charred edges, but watch that it doesn't burn too much. To serve, slice finely across the grain.

H
harusame **34,** 35
  Spring Rain Tempura **92,** 93
Hokkien noodles **8,** 9
  Chile Shrimp Noodles 125
  Curry Mee 116
  Hokkien Mee 117
  Hokkien Noodles with Shrimp 67
  Indian Mee Goreng 118
  Laksa Lemak **122,** 123
  Mee Rebus 119
  Noodles with Pork and Pickles 83
  Penang Laksa 121
  Sichuan Noodle-Shop Noodles 74
homemade noodles
  egg 186
  soba 188
  udon 187
Hor Fun Soup Noodles with Roast Duck
  52, 53

I
Indian Mee Goreng 118

K
Kalgooksu 161
Kao Soi 133
Khanom Jeen with Spicy Pork 134
Khao Pun Nam Ya 178
Korean Beef Broth 193
Korean Cucumber Pickles 193
Korean Daikon Pickles 193

L
Laksa Lemak **122,** 123
Laksa Paste 190
lamb
  Noodles with Shredded Lamb **64,** 65
Lion's Head Meatballs 66
Long-Life Noodles 58

M
Mandu Dumplings 192
Mandu Kuk 162
meatballs
  Lion's Head Meatballs 66
  Moo Sarong 135
  Nem Nuong 154, 155
  see also dumplings
Mee Krob 130, 131
Mee Rebus 119
Mee Siam 120
Memories of Shikoku Udon **96,** 97
Mohinga 174
Moo Sarong 135
Moon-Viewing Noodles 108
Mu Chungol 163
Mul Naeng Myun 164

N
Nabeyaki Udon 99

naeng myun **38,** 39
  Bibim Naeng Myun 160
  Mul Naeng Myun 164
Nam Pla Ra 191
Nem Nuong **154,** 155
Noodles with Pork and Pickles 83
Noodles with Shredded Lamb **64,** 65
Nuoc Cham (Vietnamese Dipping
  Sauce) 192

O
Odamaki Mushi 106

P
Pad Thai 136
Pad Woon Sen **138,** 139
Pancit Canton 173
Panthe Kaukswe 175
Penang Laksa 121
Pho Bo 152
Pho Ga 153
pickles
  Korean Cucumber Pickles 193
  Korean Daikon Pickles 193
  Noodles with Pork and Pickles 83
pork
  Ants Climbing Trees 71
  Brown Sauce Noodles **48,** 49
  Bun Bo Hué 148
  Char Sieu (Red Roast Pork) 189
  Dry-Cooked Green Beans with
    Noodles 81
  Khanom Jeen with Spicy Pork 134
  Lion's Head Meatballs 66
  Mee Krob **130,** 131
  Moo Sarong 135
  Nem Nuong **154,** 155
  Noodles with Pork and Pickles 83
  Pork and Rice Stick Noodle Soup 179
  Ramen with Char Sieu 107
  Roast Pork Noodle Soup 59
  Shanghai Pork Noodles **68,** 69
  Suckling Pig, Jellyfish and Noodle
    Salad 87

R
ramen **32,** 33
  Five Mushroom Miso with Ramen 111
  Ramen with Char Sieu 107
rice sheet noodles, fresh **16,** 17
  Char Kueh Teow **114,** 115
  Fried Hor Fun with Beef 57
  Gwaytio Neua Sap 132
  Hor Fun Soup Noodles with Roast
    Duck **52,** 53
  Pho Bo 152
  Pho Ga 153
rice sticks **22,** 23
  Pad Thai 136
  Pork and Rice Stick Noodle Soup 179

rice vermicelli **18,** 19
  Chicken Noodle Salad 80
  Goi Cuon (Fresh Spring Rolls) 151
  Hokkien Mee 117
  Khao Pun Nam Ya 178
  Laksa Lemak **122,** 123
  Mee Krob **130,** 131
  Mee Siam 120
  Mohinga 174
  Moo Sarong 135
  Nem Nuong **154,** 155
  Shanghai Pork Noodles **68,** 69
  Singapore Beehoon 124
  Soto Ayam 172
  Stir-Fried Pumpkin with Rice
    Vermicelli **176,** 177
  Thai Chicken Noodle Soup 142
Roast Pork Noodle Soup 59
Round Rice Noodles, Fresh **20,** 21
  Bun Bo Hué 148
  Bun Rieu Noodle Soup with Crab
    Dumplings **146,** 147
  Chile Mussels with Rice Noodles 140
  Khanom Jeen with Spicy Pork 134
  Khao Pun Nam Ya 178
  Laksa Lemak **122,** 123
  Penang Laksa 121
  Thai Chicken Noodle Soup 142

S
salads
  Beef and Glass Noodle Salad 143
  Chicken Noodle Salad 80
  Glass Noodle Som Tum 141
  Seafood and Glass Noodle Salad 137
  Suckling Pig, Jellyfish and Noodle
    Salad 87
San Choy Bau with Cellophane
  Noodles 86
sauces
  Chile Sauce 79
  Dipping Sauce 93
  Nam Pla Ra 191
  Nuoc Cham (Vietnamese Dipping
    Sauce) 192
  Spicy Sichuan Sauce 72
  teriyaki sauce 109
seafood
  Bun Rieu Noodle Soup with Crab
    Dumplings **146,** 147
  Cellophane Noodles with Shrimp 149
  Chile Mussels with Rice Noodles 140
  Chile Shrimp Noodles 125
  Char Kueh Teow **114,** 115
  Cross the Bridge Noodles 78
  Hokkien Mee 117
  Hokkien Noodles with Shrimp 67
  Kalgooksu 161
  Laksa Lemak **122,** 123
  Mee Krob **130,** 131
  Mee Siam 120

Pork and Rice Stick Noodle Soup 179
Seafood and Glass Noodle Salad 137
Spicy Squid with Somen 165
Spring Rain Tempura **92,** 93
Stir-Fried Pumpkin with Rice
  Vermicelli **176,** 177
Tempura Soba 103
sevian noodles **14,** 15
Sevian Kheer **180,** 181
Shanghai noodles **12,** 13
Brown Sauce Noodles **48,** 49
Gung Bao Chicken with Shanghai
  Noodles 82
Shanghai Pork Noodles **68,** 69
Stir-Fried Shanghai Noodles 70
shirataki **36,** 37
Sukiyaki 102
Sichuan Beef Noodle Soup 75
Sichuan Chile Oil 188
Sichuan Fish Noodles **76,** 77
Sichuan Noodle-Shop Noodles 74
Singapore Beehoon 124
soba **26,** 27
homemade 188
Soba with Eggplant and Miso 110
Tempura Soba 103
Zaru Soba **100,** 101
somen **30,** 31
Chilled Somen 94
Somen with Salt-Grilled Snapper
  104, 105
Spicy Squid with Somen 165
Soto Ayam 172
soups
Bibim Naeng Myun 160
Bun Bo Hué 148
Bun Rieu Noodle Soup with Crab
  Dumplings **146,** 147
Chicken Noodle Soup 56
Cross the Bridge Noodles 78
Eggflower Noodle Soup 50
Hor Fun Soup Noodles with Roast
  Duck **52,** 53
Mandu Kuk 162
Mohinga 174
Mu Chungol 163
Pho Bo 152
Pho Ga 153
Pork and Rice Stick Noodle Soup 179
Roast Pork Noodle Soup 59
Sichuan Beef Noodle Soup 75
Soto Ayam 172
Thai Chicken Noodle Soup 142
Wonton Soup with Noodles **60,** 61
Spicy Squid with Somen 165
Spring Rain Tempura **92,** 93
spring rolls
Cha Gio (Finger-Size Spring Rolls) 150
Goi Cuon (Fresh Spring Rolls) 151
Stir-Fried Pumpkin with Rice Vermicelli
  176, 177
Stir-Fried Shanghai Noodles 70

stock
Chinese Chicken Stock 189
Korean Beef Broth 193
Suckling Pig, Jellyfish and Noodle
  Salad 87
Sukiyaki 102

T
tempura
Spring Rain Tempura **92,** 93
Tempura Batter 191
Tempura Soba 103
Teriyaki Salmon with Udon and Spinach
  109
Thai Chicken Noodle Soup 142
Thai Red Curry Paste 191
Two-Sides-Brown Noodles with Shredded
  Duck 62

U
udon **28,** 29
Curry Udon 95
Fox Noodles with Chicken and
  Mushrooms 98
homemade 187
Memories of Shikoku Udon **96,** 97
Moon-Viewing Noodles 108
Nabeyaki Udon 99
Odamaki Mushi 106
Teriyaki Salmon with Udon and
  Spinach 109

V
vegetables
Beef and Water Spinach Noodles 54
Buddhist Vegetable Noodles 63
Dry-Cooked Green Beans with Noodles
  81
Five Mushroom Miso with Ramen 111
Fox Noodles with Chicken and
  Mushrooms 98
Soba with Eggplant and Miso 110
Spicy Squid with Vegetables and
  Noodles 165
Stir-Fried Pumpkin with Rice
  Vermicelli **176,** 177
Teriyaki Salmon with Udon and
  Spinach 109
vermicelli *see* bean thread vermicelli;
  rice vermicelli

W
wheat noodles **4,** 5
Beef and Water Spinach Noodles 54
Eight Treasure Noodles **84,** 85
Roast Pork Noodle Soup 59
Two-Sides-Brown Noodles with
  Shredded Duck 62
Wonton Soup with Noodles **60,** 61

Z
Zaru Soba **100,** 101

First published 1998 in Australia by Allen & Unwin Pty Ltd (A Sue Hines Book).
North American edition published 1999 by Soma Books, by arrangement with
Allen & Unwin.

Soma Books is an imprint of Bay Books & Tapes, 555 De Haro St., No. 220,
San Francisco, CA 94107

Photography: Geoff Lung
Book design and typesetting: Simon Johnston
North American editor: Cynthia Nims
Proofreader: Ken Della Penta

Library of Congress Cataloging-in-Publication Data
   Durack, Terry
      Noodle / Terry Durack : photography by Geoff Lung.
         p.   cm.
      Reprint. Originally published: Sydney, Australia : Allen & Unwin, 1998
      Includes bibliographical references and index.
      ISBN 1-57959-053-5 (hc : alk. paper)
      1. Cookery (Pasta) 2. Noodles. 3. Cookery, Asian. I. Title.
   TX809.N65D87 1999   99-24105
   641.8'22--dc21   CIP

ISBN 1-57959-053-5

Printed in Hong Kong
10 9 8 7 6 5 4 3 2 1

Distributed by Publishers Group West